THE BIRD ATLAS

Illustrated by Richard Orr
Written by Barbara Taylor

DK

DORLING KINDERSLEY
LONDON • NEW YORK • STUTTGART

DK

A DORLING KINDERSLEY BOOK

Project Editor Anderley Moore
Art Editor Sheilagh Noble
Designer Heather Blackham
Production Shelagh Gibson
Managing Editor Susan Peach
Managing Art Editor Jacquie Gulliver
US Editor B. Alison Weir

Bird Consultants Michael Chinery MA
Deslie Lawrence

First American Edition, 1993
10 9 8 7 6 5 4 3 2 1

Published in the United States by
Dorling Kindersley, Inc., 232 Madison Avenue
New York, New York 10016

Copyright © 1993
Dorling Kindersley Limited, London

Distributed by Houghton Mifflin Company, Boston.

CIP data is available.
ISBN 1-56458-327-9

Reproduced in Hong Kong by Bright Arts
Printed in Italy by New Interlitho, Milan

CONTENTS

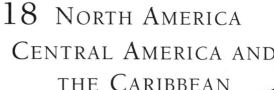

How to Use This Atlas

THE BIRD ATLAS IS ARRANGED in order of continent – the Americas, Europe, Africa, Asia, Australasia, and Antarctica. A double-page spread, such as the one on Africa (right), introduces the continent as a whole. This is followed by pages showing the main places where birds live – their habitats – within that continent.

When turning to any page, you can see which continent it is about by looking at the heading in the top left-hand corner; the habitat featured is given in the top right-hand corner. The sample pages below show how the information is presented on the two main types of pages – continental and habitat pages – and explain the maps, symbols, and abbreviations used.

CONTINENTAL PAGES

These pages introduce the continent and give an overview of the climate, landscape, main bird habitats, typical birds, and amazing birds to be found there. A large map shows the size of the continent, its position on the globe, and major geographical features. There is also usually a feature on how the position of the continent has changed over millions of years, as a result of continental drift.

WHERE ON EARTH?

The red shaded area on this globe highlights the location of the habitat featured on the page. For example, the shaded area on this globe shows the position of Central America and the Caribbean within the Americas.

BIRD SYMBOLS

Symbols of each of the birds illustrated on the page show the main areas where each species lives, although some birds live all over the region. By looking at the key, you can identify the birds and then find them on the map.

HOW BIG?

Length: 12 in (30 cm)

Labels next to each bird tell you how big it is. The length of a bird is measured from the tip of its bill to the end of the tail. Sometimes male and female birds look different from one another and are very different in size. In these cases, measurements for males and females are given separately. In special cases, the wingspan, length of tail feathers or the height of the bird may also be given. For example, on this page you can find out how big a Quetzal is and also discover the length of the male's remarkable tail feathers.

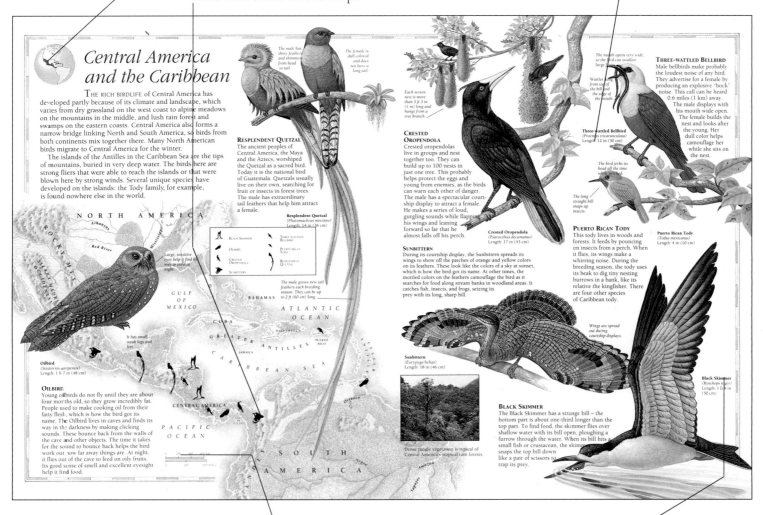

Central America and the Caribbean

THE RICH BIRDLIFE of Central America has developed partly because of its climate and landscape, which varies from dry grassland on the west coast to alpine meadows on the mountains in the middle, and lush rain forest and swamps on the eastern coasts. Central America also forms a narrow bridge linking North and South America, so birds from both continents mix together there. Many North American birds migrate to Central America for the winter.

The islands of the Antilles in the Caribbean Sea are the tips of mountains, buried in very deep water. The birds here are strong fliers that were able to reach the islands or that were blown here by strong winds. Several unique species have developed on the islands: the Tody family, for example, is found nowhere else in the world.

RESPLENDENT QUETZAL
The ancient peoples of Central America, the Maya and the Aztecs, worshiped the Quetzal as a sacred bird. Today it is the national bird of Guatemala. Quetzals usually live on their own, searching for fruit or insects in forest trees. The male has extraordinary tail feathers that help him attract a female.

Resplendent Quetzal
(*Pharomachrus mocinno*)
Length: 14 in (36 cm)

The male grows new tail feathers each breeding season. They can be up to 2 ft (60 cm) long.

CRESTED OROPENDOLA
Crested oropendolas live in groups and nest together too. They can build up to 100 nests in just one tree. This probably helps protect the eggs and young from enemies, as the birds can warn each other of danger. The male has a spectacular court-ship display to attract a female. He makes a series of loud, gurgling sounds while flapping his wings and leaning forward so far that he almost falls off his perch.

Crested Oropendola
(*Psarocolius decumanus*)
Length: 17 in (43 cm)

SUNBITTERN
During its courtship display, the Sunbittern spreads its wings to show off the patches of orange and yellow colors on its feathers. These look like the colors of a sky at sunset, which is how the bird got its name. At other times, the mottled colors on the feathers camouflage the bird as it searches for food along stream banks in woodland areas. It catches fish, insects, and frogs, seizing its prey with its long, sharp bill.

Sunbittern
(*Eurypyga helias*)
Length: 18 in (46 cm)

Dense jungle vegetation is typical of Central America's tropical rain forests.

THREE-WATTLED BELLBIRD
Male bellbirds make probably the loudest noise of any bird. They advertise for a female by producing an explosive "bock" noise. This call can be heard 0.6 miles (1 km) away. The male displays with his mouth wide open. The female builds the nest and looks after the young. Her dull color helps camouflage her while she sits on the nest.

Three-wattled Bellbird
(*Procnias tricarunculata*)
Length: 12 in (30 cm)

PUERTO RICAN TODY
This tody lives in woods and forests. It feeds by pouncing on insects from a perch. When it flies, its wings make a whirring noise. During the breeding season, the tody uses its beak to dig tiny nesting burrows in a bank, like its relative the kingfisher. There are four other species of Caribbean tody.

Puerto Rican Tody
(*Todus mexicanus*)
Length: 4 in (10 cm)

BLACK SKIMMER
The Black Skimmer has a strange bill – the bottom part is about one-third longer than the top part. To find food, the skimmer flies over shallow water with its bill open, ploughing a furrow through the water. When its bill hits a small fish or crustacean, the skimmer snaps the top bill down like a pair of scissors to trap its prey.

Black Skimmer
(*Rhynchops niger*)
Length: 1 ft 8 in (50 cm)

OILBIRD
Young oilbirds do not fly until they are about four months old, so they grow incredibly fat. People used to make cooking oil from their fatty flesh, which is how the bird got its name. The Oilbird lives in caves and finds its way in the darkness by making clicking sounds. These bounce back from the walls of the cave and other objects. The time it takes for the sound to bounce back helps the bird work out how far away things are. At night, it flies out of the cave to feed on oily fruits. Its good sense of smell and excellent eyesight help it find food.

Oilbird
(*Steatornis caripensis*)
Length: 1 ft 7 in (48 cm)

SCALE
You can use this scale to work out the size of the area shown on the map.

LATIN NAMES

Black Skimmer
Rhynchops niger

Scientists have given each species of bird a Latin name. This means that people from all over the world can use the same name to identify birds, no matter what language they speak. A bird's Latin name is divided into two parts. The first name is a group name given to a number of similar birds. For example, *Rhynchops* is the group name, or genus, for skimmers. The second part of the name identifies the particular species of bird and often tells you something more specific about it. In this case it is *niger*, the Latin word for black.

ABBREVIATIONS USED IN THE ATLAS:

Imperial		Metric	
in	inch	mm	millimeter
ft	foot	cm	centimeter
mph	miles per hour	m	meter
sq miles	square miles	km	kilometer
lb	pound	sq km	square kilometers
F	fahrenheit	kph	kilometers per hour
		kg	kilogram
		C	centigrade

What is a Bird?

BIRDS ARE THE ONLY ANIMALS in the world that have feathers. They also lay eggs, breathe air, and keep their body temperature the same all the time. This is called being warm-blooded. Birds developed or evolved from reptiles about 150 million years ago. The earliest bird we know of, *Archaeopteryx* (meaning ancient wing), lived at this time. It was about the size of a crow and had feathers, although it probably couldn't fly very well. From early birds like *Archaeopteryx*, the 9,000 or so species of bird alive today have developed.

Archaeopteryx

Body or contour feather from a Red Lory

Down feather from a pigeon

Flight feather from a Guinea Fowl

FEATHERS

A bird has a vast number of feathers. Even a small bird, such as a wren, has more than 1,000 feathers. There are three main types of feather – flight feathers on the wings and tail, body feathers to cover the body and give a bird its shape, and fluffy down feathers to keep it warm. Flight feathers are made of strands called barbs that hook together. If the hooks come apart, they can be drawn together again, like zipping up. Each year, a bird sheds or molts most of its old feathers and grows new ones to replace them.

Peregrine Falcon
(*Falco peregrinus*)

A bird's wing is light, strong, and flexible, so it will not snap as the bird twists and turns through the air.

BIRD BONES

A bird has a bony skeleton inside its body to support and protect delicate organs, such as its heart, lungs, and brain. But the whole skeleton of flying birds is very light, and the long bones in their wings and legs are hollow, with a honeycomb of stiff supporting struts (above). This means they have less weight to lift off the ground and keep up in the air.

A bird uses its tail feathers for steering as it flies through the air.

The bill is lightweight, but very strong; birds do not have teeth.

Rock Dove
(*Columba livia*)

Pigeons and many other birds have a flapping flight. Others, such as eagles and albatrosses, glide long distances without flapping their wings much. Hummingbirds and kestrels can hover.

Birds have scaly legs like those of their reptile ancestors.

HOW BIRDS FLY

Birds are the largest, fastest, and most powerful flying animals alive. They have a smooth, streamlined shape to cut through the air easily, their front limbs are wings to push them along, and they have powerful chest muscles to help them flap their wings up and down. A bird's wings are curved on top and flat underneath. As a bird flies, this airfoil shape creates an area of high air pressure under the wing and an area of low air pressure above it. The high pressure under the wing pushes the bird up into the air. Some birds, such as penguins and ostriches, cannot fly; they run or swim very fast instead.

EGGS AND CHICKS

All birds lay eggs. The hard eggshell protects the developing chick, and there is a food store inside the egg. Air can pass through the eggshell to reach the developing chick inside. While the chick develops, the parents have to keep the eggs warm by sitting on them. This is called incubation. Many birds are blind, featherless, and helpless when they hatch. Other birds, such as this duckling, stay longer inside the egg, so they are better developed when they hatch. They can run about and fend for themselves almost as soon as they come out of their shell.

BIRD BILLS

Birds use their bills to catch and hold their food, care for their feathers, and build nests. The size and shape of a bird's bill depend on what it eats and where it finds its food.

Pine Grosbeak
(*Pinicola enucleator*)
Seed-eater

Small Green Barbet
(*Megalaima viridis*)
Fruit and insect-eater

African Paradise Flycatcher
(*Terpsiphone viridis*)
Insect-eater

Australian Darter
(*Anhinga novaehollandiae*)
Fish-eater

A duckling starts to break out of its shell by cutting a circle with its bill.

When the young bird pushes itself out of the shell, its feathers are still wet.

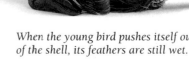

Within three hours its feathers are dry and fluffy, and it can run around.

Where Birds Live

BIRDS LIVE IN EVERY CORNER OF THE GLOBE. They have spread so far because they can fly from one place to another, live on a variety of foods, and maintain a constant body temperature in most types of weather.

The place in which a bird lives is called its habitat. This is rather like its "home address." A bird's habitat must provide food, shelter, and somewhere to nest. Some birds, such as the Barn Owl, can live in a range of habitats from woodland to scrub; others are more specialized (toucans, for example, live only in the rain forests of Central and South America). Some birds stay permanently in one habitat, while others move away – migrate – at certain times of year. There are an increasing number of human-made habitats, such as houses, parks, and gardens. Some of the most common birds, such as starlings and sparrows, have adapted to live in these new habitats near people.

The main types of bird habitat around the world are shown at the bottom of these pages.

LOOK-ALIKES

Birds have developed in different ways according to the habitat in which they live and the food they eat. The map below shows the world's grasslands and three birds that look similar because they have all adapted to live in similar grassland habitats. This is known as convergent evolution. The ostrich, the emu, and the rhea are probably related, but there are other examples of convergent evolution where the birds are not related at all. For example, the toucans of South America look like the hornbills of Africa and Asia, although they do not belong to the same family.

Emu
(Dromaius novaehollandiae)
Australia

Greater Rhea
(Rhea americana)
South America

Ostrich
(Struthio camelus)
Africa

NORTH AMERICA
EUROPE
ASIA
AFRICA
SOUTH AMERICA
AUSTRALIA
ATLANTIC OCEAN
PACIFIC OCEAN
INDIAN OCEAN

POLAR AND TUNDRA
The Arctic in the north and the Antarctic in the south are among the harshest environments on Earth. Freezing temperatures, howling gales, and long dark winters mean that few birds can live there, but seabirds nest along the coasts in summer. Surrounding the Arctic is a cold, treeless region called the tundra. In summer, birds such as waders, ducks, and geese flock there to raise their young because of few enemies, plenty of food, and light all the time.

Find out more: pages 8-9, 58-59

CONIFEROUS FOREST

Coniferous trees such as pine, fir, and spruce grow in a huge forest called the taiga, which stretches across the top of North America, Europe, and Asia. The taiga is one of the largest forest areas in the world. Most coniferous trees have needle-like leaves that stay on the trees all year round. Birds feed on the tree cones and help spread the tree seeds. Summers are usually mild, but winters are bitterly cold. Many birds fly south to warmer places in winter.

Find out more: pages 12-13, 28-29

DECIDUOUS WOODLANDS

Deciduous, or broad-leaved, woodlands grow south of the dark conifer woods. Many of the trees, such as oak and beech, lose their leaves in winter, but there is plenty of rainfall all year round, and the climate is generally mild. These woodlands provide plenty of food and nesting places for birds in spring and summer.

Find out more: pages 12-13, 52-53

GRASSLANDS

Grasslands occur where the climate is too dry and the soil is too poor for most trees to survive. Fires are common in this habitat, but the grasses grow back. Grasslands provide plenty of food for seed- and insect-eating birds. Tropical grasslands, such as the African savannah, are hot all year round with long dry spells. Temperate grasslands such as the South American pampas, are cooler, with hot summers and long, cold winters.

Find out more: pages 23, 38-39

ISLAND EVOLUTION

Many rare and unusual birds live on islands, such as the Hawaiian Islands (shown below), the Galapagos Islands, Madagascar, and Japan. These species have developed in unique ways because they have been cut off from their relatives on the mainland for a long time. For example, on the Hawaiian Islands, a finch-like bird arrived some 15-20 million years ago. Since there were few other birds to compete with it, this bird evolved into more than 40 different species called honeycreepers (p.11). Each species found its own type of habitat and food so could live alongside other honeycreepers.

MOUNTAIN HABITATS

Mountains such as the Himalayas in Asia (right), the Andes in South America, the Rockies in North America, and the Alps in Europe provide a wide range of bird habitats. The lower slopes have warm forests, but these merge into grasslands and tundra higher up. Above a certain height – called the tree line – there are no trees because it is too cold for them to grow. Near the very top, the ground is covered with

snow and ice, and no birds can live there. Mountain birds have to cope with freezing temperatures, fierce winds, and thin air. Some birds move up and down the mountains with the seasons.

LIVING TOGETHER

In any one habitat, different species of bird live side by side. In a rich habitat, such as a deciduous woodland, various kinds of bird can live on a single tree by feeding and nesting at different levels and eating different types or sizes of food. Some eat insects, while others prefer seeds. In this way, the birds share out the resources of the habitat and are more likely to survive than if they compete with each other for the same things.

Near the top of the tree, tiny birds such as blue tits and wood warblers hang from the smaller twigs and pick insects off the leaves and bark.

In the middle of the tree, birds such as Spotted Flycatchers dart out from a perch to catch flying insects. Woodpeckers chisel into trunks and branches to find insects. They also dig out nesting holes in the trunk.

On the woodland floor, bigger birds such as the woodcock feed and nest. These birds are usually well camouflaged among the dead leaves. Wrens and other small insect-eaters hop nimbly through the dense thickets of leaves and twigs, where they are hidden from enemies.

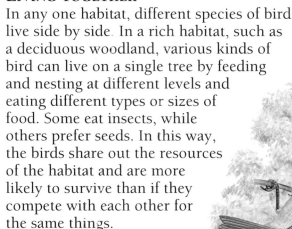

Wood Warbler
(*Phylloscopus sibilatrix*)

Blue Tit
(*Parus caerulus*)

Great Spotted Woodpecker
(*Dendrocopus major*)

Spotted Flycatcher
(*Muscicapa striata*)

Woodcock
(*Scopolax rusticola*)

Wren
(*Troglodytes troglodytes*)

SCRUBLANDS

This warm, dry, dusty habitat with tough shrubs and small trees is found mainly around the shores of the Mediterranean Sea, California, and parts of Australia, where it is called the outback or the bush. Many birds move, or migrate, to these scrublands during the long, hot summers, when there are plenty of insects and seeds to feed on. Some fly away for the cooler, wetter winter months.

Find out more: pages 30-31, 52-53

DESERTS

Deserts cover about one-fifth of the Earth's land surface. They are a difficult habitat for birds because there is little rainfall and daytime temperatures are very high. Birds have to rest in the shade during the hottest times of day and either get water from their food or fly long distances to find it. Important deserts of the world include the western deserts of North America, the Sahara, Kalahari, and Namib deserts in Africa, and the Australian deserts.

Find out more: pages 15, 52-53

RAIN FORESTS

Rain forests grow near the Equator where it is hot and wet all year round. They cover less than 10 percent of the Earth's surface but are home to more than half of all the different species of wildlife living on Earth. Many birds live high up in the treetops, where there is more sunlight, warmth, and food. But birds live at all levels in the forest, sharing out the food and space of this rich habitat.The largest birds live on the forest floor.

Find out more: pages 20-21, 36-37, 54-55

WETLANDS

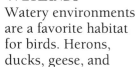

Watery environments are a favorite habitat for birds. Herons, ducks, geese, and swans flock to wetlands because there are plenty of fish, insects, and water plants for them to eat as well as reeds and riverbanks for them to nest in. Trees grow in swampy areas, but there are seldom any trees on marshland. Drainage and pollution of their wetland habitats by people is a major threat to many of these birds.

Find out more: pages 16-17, 40-41

The Arctic

THE ARCTIC REGION lies right at the top of the world. It is mainly a huge ice-covered ocean, but it also includes the northern edges of North America, Europe, Asia, and Greenland. The ice-free land in the Arctic has a low, flat tundra landscape, with many lichens, mosses, grasses, bushes, and sprawling ground-hugging bushes.

Few birds can live in the Arctic all year round because it is so cold, particularly in winter, when it is also dark all day and all night. During the few light summer months, many birds migrate to the Arctic to nest and feed. At this time of year, microscopic sea plants and animals grow fast in the light and warmth of the sea. They are eaten by fish, which in turn provide food for millions of gulls, auks, and terns. On the tundra lands, some of the ice melts, flowers make seeds, and insects hatch. Waders, ducks, geese, and smaller birds hurry to eat the seeds or insects, lay their eggs, and raise their young before flying south to escape the harsh Arctic winter.

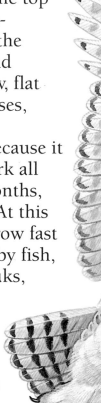

SNOWY OWL

Like a silent white ghost, the Snowy Owl glides over the Arctic tundra, hunting for birds and small mammals, such as lemmings and hares. It will sometimes kill as many as 10 lemmings a day. When there is plenty of food around, these powerful owls lay lots of eggs, so that their chicks have a good chance of survival. When food is scarce, they may not bother to nest at all.

Snowy Owl
(*Nyctea scandiaca*)
Length: 2 ft 3 in (68 cm)

The female is larger than the male and has more black markings.

Food is carried in a pouch, or crop. This makes the throat bulge out.

Powerful legs and talons attack and carry off heavy prey.

The male's summer breeding plumage helps him attract a female. He becomes much paler than this in winter.

LAPLAND BUNTING

In the summer months, the Lapland Bunting, or Longspur, migrates to the Arctic tundra to nest. There are no trees in the tundra for it to perch on while it sings to attract females or ward off rival males. Instead, it has to stand on rocks or fly up in the air to sing. It often nests in small groups for protection from predators.

Lapland Bunting
(*Calcarius lapponicus*)
Length: 6 in (15.5 cm)

DOVEKIE

These tiny birds look like the penguins of the Antarctic because they live and feed in a similar way. Their bodies are streamlined for swimming underwater and they use their flipper-like wings to push them along. A thick layer of fat under the skin keeps them warm in the cold Arctic seas. Millions of dovekies, or little auks, as they are also called, raise their young on the Arctic coasts in summer. In winter, they move south, but they do not often go far south of the Arctic Circle.

Dovekie
(*Alle alle*)
Length: 8 in (20 cm)

LONG-TAILED DUCK

In the Arctic summer, the yodeling courtship call of male long-tailed ducks carries great distances across the open tundra landscape. Some birdwatchers think the call sounds like bagpipes being played. Long-tailed ducks are very good at diving and can plunge as deep as 180 ft (55 m) to chase and catch fish. In shallow water, they take shellfish and other small animals from the muddy bottom.

The female has dark cheek patches.

The male has long tail feathers.

Long-tailed Duck
(*Clangula hyemalis*)
Length: 1 ft 7 in (47 cm)

The summer plumage of the male and female is mainly brown with white patches. In winter, it is the opposite way around – mainly white with brown patches.

Map legend

Snowy Owl	Long-tailed Duck
Lapland Bunting	Red-necked Phalarope
Arctic Tern	
Dovekie	Tundra Swan

Map labels: CHUKCHI SEA, BEAUFORT SEA, NORTH AMERICA, VICTORIA ISLAND, ELLESMERE ISLAND, BAFFIN ISLAND, BAFFIN BAY, GREENLAND, ICELAND, ARCTIC CIRCLE, GREENLAND SEA, ARCTIC OCEAN (permanently frozen), SVALBARD, BARENTS SEA, FRANZ JOSEF LAND, KARA SEA, LAPTEV SEA, ASIA, EUROPE

Scale: 0 300 600 900 km / 0 300 600 miles

In the tundra, the ground is always frozen just below the surface. A thin layer of soil above it freezes in winter and melts in summer. Water collects on the surface, forming lakes and swamps where waterbirds can feed.

Arctic Tern
(*Sterna paradisaea*)
Length: 15 in (38 cm)

A male tern brings his mate a gift of fish during courtship. This food gives the female the extra energy she needs to form eggs.

ARCTIC TERN

These graceful and elegant fliers travel farther than any other bird and see more hours of daylight each year than any other creature. Arctic terns raise their young during the Arctic summer. When autumn arrives, they fly down to the Antarctic, where summer is just beginning. This involves a round trip of about 22,000 miles (36,000 km) each year. They nest in large colonies and help each other drive away attackers. They dive-bomb enemies such as Arctic foxes or peck at their heads.

TUNDRA SWAN

These swans, also known as Bewick's swans, nest in the Arctic but migrate long distances to spend the winter in Europe, China, Japan, and the United States. The young swans, called cygnets, migrate with their parents when they are only about three months old. Females lay their eggs in a nest of moss and sedge on marshy ground near water. The nest is usually lined with down feathers, which the female plucks from her breast to keep the eggs warm.

Male and female Tundra swans look exactly the same.

Each bird has different yellow markings on its bill.

Tundra Swan
(*Cygnus columbianus*)
Length: 4 ft (1.2 m)

RED-NECKED PHALAROPE

This is an unusual bird because the female has more brightly colored feathers than the male and takes the lead during courtship. In most other birds, it is the male that looks and behaves this way. The male Red-necked Phalarope also sits on the eggs and takes care of the chicks. They can fend for themselves after about three weeks. When the Arctic winter sets in, red-necked phalaropes migrate south to warmer places. Look for phalaropes spinning like tops on the water.

Red-necked Phalarope
(*Phalaropus lobatus*)
Length: 7 in (18 cm)

A male looks after the chicks, which are striped for camouflage.

9

The Americas

THE AMERICAS ARE MADE UP of two of the largest continents in the world – North America and South America. North America includes the Caribbean islands and Central America – the narrow strip of mountainous land that links the two continents.

South America is generally warmer than North America and contains the greatest variety of bird species on Earth. It was cut off from the other continents for millions of years and many of its birds, such as the Hoatzin, Oilbird, rheas, and trumpeters, are found nowhere else.

Almost half the world's bird species either breed in the tropical rain forests of South America or visit them on migration.

By contrast, North America has no unique species, and its bird life is less varied. One reason for this is the large number of cities and farms in the region, but the colder climate is also important. Less food and shelter are available, and many birds have to migrate to Central and South America during the cold season. Also, the last ice ages wiped out many North American birds or drove them south.

CONTINENTS ON THE MOVE

The Earth's thin surface layer, or crust, is made up of several gigantic pieces called plates, which float on a much thicker layer of liquid rock underneath them. Powerful forces within the Earth move the plates slowly around the globe, carrying the world's great landmasses, or continents, with them. This movement is known as continental drift. The continents of North and South America have not always been in the position they are in today. Over millions of years, continental drift has pulled the two continents apart and pushed them together again, altering their shape and landscape.

About 200 million years ago all the continents formed one landmass called Pangaea, but this was slowly beginning to break apart.

About 50 million years ago North America had separated from Europe and Asia, and South America was an island on its own. Many unique and unusual birds evolved in South America because the birds could not mix with those far away on other continents.

About 3 million years ago the continents had moved into the positions found on our world map today. South America had joined onto North America. Birds could use the Central American land bridge to move north and south between the two continents.

AMAZING BIRDS OF THE AMERICAS

Tiniest bird
The Cuban Bee Hummingbird is the smallest bird in the world. An adult male is only 2.2 in (5.7 cm) long.

Slowest flight
The American Woodcock flies incredibly slowly for a bird, at 5 mph (8 kph).

Fastest spread
In 1890, 120 European starlings were introduced to New York. Within only 60 years, they spread across most of North America.

Heaviest nest
The Bald Eagle builds the largest nest of any bird. A single nest can weigh 4,400 lb (2,000 kg), about the same as two army jeeps.

Deepest dive
The Great Northern Diver is the deepest diving bird; it dives up to 266 ft (81 m).

Quickest runner
The Greater Roadrunner is the fastest-running flying bird. It runs up to 18 mph (29 kph).

CLIMATE AND LANDSCAPE

The Americas stretch across the whole globe, from the Arctic in the north almost down to Antarctica in the south. All the major habitats in the world can be found there, including dark evergreen forests, sunny broad-leaved woodlands, dry grasslands, humid rain forests, deserts, and swamps. Two huge mountain ranges – the Rockies and the Andes – stretch down the western side of the region and keep birds from moving freely from east to west.

ARCTIC OCEAN

HUDSON BAY

NORTH AMERICA

GULF OF ALASKA

ROCKY MTS

Great Lakes

Mississippi

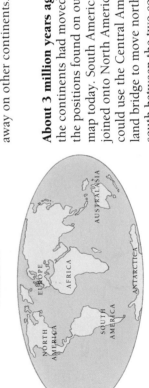

Heavy storms occur in the Caribbean Sea in late summer. They can blow birds off course during their migration from North America.

PANGAEA

ASIA
EUROPE
AFRICA
AUSTRALASIA
ANTARCTICA
NORTH AMERICA
SOUTH AMERICA

EUROPE
ASIA
AFRICA
AUSTRALASIA
ANTARCTICA
NORTH AMERICA
SOUTH AMERICA

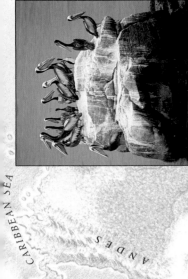

Number of birds
More than 3,100 species of bird live in South America. Colombia alone has more than 1,700 breeding species. Only about 650 species of bird live and breed in North America north of Mexico.

Largest lake
Lake Superior is the largest of the Great Lakes of North America and the largest freshwater lake in the world.

FACTS ABOUT THE AMERICAS

Longest mountains
The Andes are the longest mountain chain on Earth, stretching for more than 4,500 miles (7,250 km) down the western side of South America.

Long river
The Amazon in South America is the second longest river in the world, after the Nile. One-fifth of all the fresh water on Earth flows through it each day. The river pours into the Atlantic Ocean with such force that it is possible to scoop up a glass of fresh water 200 miles (320 km) out to sea.

Highest waterfall
The Angel Falls in Venezuela are the highest in the world at 3,212 ft (979 m).

Highest temperature
Death Valley in North America is one of the hottest places on Earth. Summer temperatures are often higher than 131°F (55°C).

Oldest mountains
The Appalachians are some of the oldest mountains in the world, formed more than 250 million years ago.

TYPICAL BIRDS
Here are just a few examples of typical birds from the most important habitats of the Americas. You can find out more about them on the next few pages.

Deserts
All the wrens in the world except for one species live in the Americas. The Cactus Wren prefers a desert habitat.

Mountains
Guans, such as the shy Andean guan, live mainly in the mountain forests of Central and South America.

Grasslands
The Burrowing Owl lives on the grasslands and deserts of the Americas. Nearly 60 species of owl live in the Americas, including screech owls and pygmy owls.

Woodlands
Crows, magpies, and jays, such as the noisy Blue Jay, are common in the woods of North America. More than 30 species of jay live in the Americas.

Islands
The Akiapolaau is one of more than 40 species of honeycreeper that live only on the Hawaiian islands.

Rain forests
Nearly 40 species of toucan, toucanet, and aracari live only in American rain forests. The Toco Toucan is a common species.

Rivers, lakes, and swamps
Perching ducks, such as the Wood Duck, nest in tree holes near water. Other typical ducks of the Americas include whistling ducks, steamer ducks, teal, eider, and scoter.

Millions of pelicans and other sea birds nest off the west coast of South America. People collect their droppings (guano) for fertilizer.

SOUTH AMERICA

PAMPAS

Amazon

ANDES

ANDES

CENTRAL AMERICA

CARIBBEAN SEA

PACIFIC OCEAN

ATLANTIC OCEAN

Forests and Woodlands

A HUGE EXPANSE OF evergreen forest stretches right across Canada, in a broad belt up to about 500 miles (800 km) wide. It is sometimes called the boreal forest – after Boreas, the Greek god of the North Wind. The cones, buds, and needles of conifer trees, such as pines, spruces, and firs, provide food for a variety of birds, such as grosbeaks, juncos, and crossbills. But the weather is bitterly cold in winter, and many birds fly south to escape the harsh climate.

To the south of these dark forests are areas of woodland where the climate is warmer and moister. The most common trees are broad-leaved species, such as oak, maple, walnut, and hickory, which lose their leaves in winter. The carpet of decaying leaves is full of insects that birds can feed on. There is also a greater variety of nesting places in these sunlit woodlands than in the dark conifer forests farther north.

BALD EAGLE

The national bird of the United States, the Bald Eagle, has a spectacular courtship display. A male and a female lock talons together and somersault through the air. The pair build a gigantic nest called an "eyrie." It is built in a tree or on a rocky cliff and is made of sticks, weeds, and soil. The eagles use the same nest every year and add to it.

The white feathers on its head are fully visible by the time the bird is four years old.

Fish such as salmon are a common source of food for the eagle.

Bald Eagle
(*Haliaeetus leucocephalus*)
Length: 2 ft 8 in (81 cm)
Wingspan: up to 7 ft 2 in
(2.2 m)

The maple trees of broad-leaved woodlands turn spectacular shades of red and gold before shedding their leaves in the fall.

YELLOW-BELLIED SAPSUCKER

The Yellow-bellied Sapsucker drills neat rows of holes in trees, such as birches, and waits for the sap to ooze out and run down the trunk. Then it laps up the sugary sap with its brushlike tongue. Insects sometimes get trapped in the sticky liquid, and the sapsucker eats these up as well. In winter, the Yellow-bellied Sapsucker migrates south to the warmer climates of Central America and the Caribbean islands.

Yellow-bellied Sapsucker
(*Sphyrapicus varius*)
Length: 8 in (20.5 cm)

The sapsucker presses its tail against the tree trunk to prop itself up.

If a covey is disturbed, the birds fly off in different directions, to confuse enemies and give the birds time to escape.

Northern Bobwhite
(*Colinus virginianus*)
Length: 10 in (25 cm)

NORTHERN BOBWHITE

Outside the breeding season, bobwhites gather in groups of 15 to 30 birds, called coveys. Each covey defends its own special area from other coveys. At night, a covey huddles on the ground in a circle. The birds sit with their heads pointing outward to face danger and their bodies touching to keep warm.

ARCTIC OCEAN

GULF OF ALASKA

Great Bear Lake

Great Slave Lake

N O R T H
A M E R I C A

P A C I F I C   O C E A N

R O C K Y   M T S

Rio Grande

| | 0 | 250 | 500 | 750 km |
| | 0 | 250 | | 500 miles |

YELLOW-BELLIED SAPSUCKER	NORTHERN CARDINAL
WHIP-POOR-WILL	BALD EAGLE
RUFFED GROUSE	AMERICAN ROBIN
NORTHERN BOBWHITE	

OWLS — THE NIGHT HUNTERS

Owls are one of the most characteristic birds of woodland areas. They have short, rounded wings, so they can fly easily between the trees. Most owls are night hunters, using their keen hearing and eyesight to catch food in the dark. They have large eyes and can turn their heads right around to see behind them. Owls collect sounds in their round faces and funnel them toward their ear openings. They have big ear openings under feathered flaps of skin on the sides of the face.

Owls have powerful legs with needle-sharp, curved talons for gripping prey.

Light feathers have a soft fringe, to break up the flow of air and muffle the sound of the wings. Owls make very little noise as they fly.

The owl's outer toe can point either forward or backward for extra grip.

The woodland owl swoops silently down from a perch, swinging its feet forward at the last minute to grab its prey. It swallows it whole, but it cannot digest bones, fur, or feathers, so it coughs these up in the form of pellets. You can find these near conifers.

NORTHERN CARDINAL

Cardinals have a rich variety of songs, and males and females, may sing in turn, as if replying to each other. Unlike other birds that live in territories just for the breeding season, cardinals sing all year round to keep other birds away. The cardinal is named after the bright red robes worn by Roman Catholic cardinals.

The male cardinal is far more colorful than the female.

During display, neck ruffs extend and tail spreads out like a fan.

RUFFED GROUSE

In spring, the male Ruffed Grouse often sits on a log and makes a drumming sound by beating his wings to and fro. The sound gets faster and faster, carrying a long way through the forest and helping to attract a female. She nests among aspen trees, feeding on the tree catkins while she sits on her eggs to keep them warm. In winter, the Ruffed Grouse grows comblike bristles on its toes, which act as snowshoes.

The male beats his wings to attract a mate.

Northern Cardinal
(Cardinalis cardinalis)
Length: 9 in (22 cm)

Mottled feathers ensure that the bird is well camouflaged among dead leaves.

Ruffed Grouse
(Bonasa umbellus)
Length: 17 in (43 cm)

Whip-poor-will
(Caprimulgus vociferus)
Length: 10 in (25 cm)

WHIP-POOR-WILL

During the day, the Whip-poor-will sleeps on the forest floor. Its mottled colors match the dead leaves, so it is hard to see. At night, it flies close to the ground with its mouth open, scooping up flying insects. The bird is so named because of its call, which sounds like "whip-poor-will." It may repeat the call a hundred times or more without stopping.

HUDSON BAY

St. Lawrence

ATLANTIC OCEAN

Great Lakes

APPALACHIAN MTS.

Mississippi

AMERICAN ROBIN

The robin originally nested in open woodlands, but it has adapted well to suburban gardens. It often builds a nest on a house porch or in a nearby tree. It eats insects and worms and also likes fruit, especially in winter. It sometimes spends the winter in northern conifer forests, gathering in large roosts of thousands of birds.

Keen eyesight helps it find worms.

American Robin
(Turdus migratorius)
Length: 10 in (25 cm)

Western Mountains

THE WESTERN MOUNTAIN RANGES, such as the Rockies, the Cascade ranges, and the Sierra Nevada, provide a variety of habitats for birds, concentrated in a small space. The warm, wet weather on the lower mountain slopes encourages the growth of dense forests. These forests shelter and feed many birds, from woodpeckers and nutcrackers to jays and chickadees. Higher up the mountains, it is cooler and drier, and the forests give way to grassy meadows and bare, rocky ground on the frozen peaks. Here, eagles and other birds of prey soar aloft on rising air currents, which sweep over the mountains. A few unusual birds, such as ptarmigans, survive on the higher slopes; their downy feathers keep them warm.

Golden Eagle
(Aquila chrysaetos)
Length: up to
3 ft 3 in (1 m)
Wingspan: up to
6 ft 6 in (2 m)

The powerful, hooked bill tears flesh from prey.

The eagle has strong talons.

GOLDEN EAGLE

To hunt for food, the Golden Eagle soars high up in the sky on its powerful wings. When its sharp eyes spot a small mammal, it dives down quickly to seize its prey and crush it in its hooked talons. The Golden Eagle will attack animals as big as deer, especially in winter. It nests on rocky crags or in tall trees; the nest of sticks can be enormous.

BLACK-BILLED MAGPIE

The Black-billed Magpie is an adaptable bird that eats a range of foods, especially insects and small rodents. It often perches on the backs of cattle and sheep to pick off the ticks and maggots that live on its skin. It builds a large, strong nest of twigs, mud, and plant material lined with fine grass and hair. A dome of sticks, often thorny ones, protects the top of the nest from enemies.

Black-billed Magpie
(Pica pica)
Length: 20 in (50 cm)

The tail is longer than the body.

Vast areas of coniferous forest at the base of the Rockies shelter less hardy birds from harsh weather.

WHITE-TAILED PTARMIGAN

In winter, this ptarmigan grows white feathers, which camouflage it against the snowy landscape. It often crouches down in the snow to keep out of the fierce, cold mountain winds and avoid enemies. It tends to run away from danger instead of flying. During the summer breeding season, it grows mottled brown feathers. These are very useful to the female, as they hide her while she is sitting on her eggs.

White-tailed Ptarmigan
(Lagopus leucurus)
Length: 12 in (32 cm)

MOUNTAIN CHICKADEE

In spring and summer, the Mountain Chickadee nests in the mountain forests, but it moves down to warmer valleys during the cold winter months. There it joins flocks of other small birds, such as warblers and vireos, which move around the valley forests searching for food. If chickadees kept to their own territories in winter, they would not find enough food to eat.

Mountain Chickadee
(Parus gambeli)
Length: 6 in (15 cm)

Feathered feet keep it warm. Scales on toes act as snowshoes to stop bird from sinking into snow.

The chickadee feeds on insects and seeds in conifers, such as this Douglas fir.

Deserts

THE HOT, DRY DESERTS of the southwestern United States are home to a surprising variety of birds. To cope with the heat, birds rest in the shade of rocks or inside burrows dug by desert mammals. Long legs also help birds lose heat. There is little water to drink – the Mojave and Sonoran Deserts receive less than 8 in (20 cm) of rain each year and the Great Basin Desert only less than 2 in (5 cm) each year. Birds are forced to get most of the water they need from their food, such as seeds, other animals, and water-filled cacti. The spiny branches of cacti help protect the nests of many birds. It is much cooler inside the cactus, out of the heat of the sun. There are few cacti in the Great Basin Desert, but the many sagebrush bushes are rich in energy-giving fats for birds to eat.

A Gila Woodpecker perches on a giant desert cactus to feed insects to its young nesting inside

CACTUS WREN

This is the largest North American wren. Like other wrens, it builds several nests – some to sleep in, some to shelter in, and a few for the eggs and young. The nests are dome-shaped with a tunnel-like entrance and are built on a prickly cholla cactus or a spiny yucca or mesquite tree. The wren doesn't seem to mind the sharp spines, but enemies find it hard to reach the nest.

Cactus Wren
(*Campylorhynchus brunneicapillus*)
Length: 8 in (21 cm)

GREATER ROADRUNNER

The roadrunner is really a type of cuckoo that lives on the ground. This shy bird is often seen on roads but runs rapidly away from danger and chases anything that moves. On its long, powerful legs, it can sprint at up to 15 mph (24 kph), fluttering its stubby wings for extra speed. Its long tail acts as a brake or rudder to help the bird stop or change direction.

Elf Owl
Microthene whitneyi
Length: 6 in (14 cm)

ELF OWL

This is the smallest owl in the world – no bigger than an adult's hand. It feeds mainly at night, catching insects with its feet. It will also eat scorpions, taking out the stinger or crushing it before starting to eat. It roosts by day in holes in giant cacti dug by other birds, to escape the heat of the sun. If captured, the Elf Owl pretends to be dead until it thinks the danger has passed.

Greater Roadrunner
(*Geococcyx californianus*)
Length: 2 ft (61 cm)

The roadrunner eats lizards, gophers, mice, scorpions, insects, and small rattlesnakes.

GULF OF ALASKA

NORTH AMERICA

ROCKY MTS

HUDSON BAY

PACIFIC OCEAN

0   200   400   600 km

0   200   400 miles

GREAT BASIN

DEATH VALLEY

MOJAVE DESERT

ROCKY MTS

GREAT PLAINS

Arkansas

Red River

SONORAN DESERT

SIERRA MADRE OCCIDENTAL

GULF OF CALIFORNIA

Rio Grande

GULF OF MEXICO

GOLDEN EAGLE		ELF OWL
BLACK-BILLED MAGPIE		CACTUS WREN
MOUNTAIN CHICKADEE		WHITE-TAILED PTARMIGAN
		GREATER ROADRUNNER

The Wetlands

THE RIVERS, LAKES, MARSHES, and swamps of North America, or wetlands as they are known, are a rich habitat for birds because of the variety of food and nesting places they provide. Many marshes were protected so people could hunt the ducks and geese, but they are now wildlife refuges. In the Southeast are swamps dominated by bald cypress trees heaped with vines, Spanish moss, and orchids. These include the bayous of the Mississippi delta and the Florida Everglades. An amazing number of ponds and lakes are scattered over North America. Some formed at the end of the Ice Age, a million years ago, where ice sheets dug hollows in the land. Others formed as a result of movements of the Earth's crust. Many North American wetlands are threatened by the pollution and drainage caused by farms and factories.

Head and neck are stretched forward, and feet are straight out behind.

Wingtips are jet black.

WHOOPING CRANE

The Whooping Crane is one of the world's most endangered species. It almost died out during the 1940s, but its numbers are slowly increasing, thanks to conservation. It nests in northwestern Canada but migrates south to the warmer weather of the Texas coastline in winter. Its name comes from its loud, trumpeting call. Whooping cranes mate for life; they are very attentive parents.

Whooping Crane
(Grus americana)
Length: 4 ft 3 in (1.3 m)

COMMON LOON

The Common Loon, or diver, as it is sometimes known, plunges up to 266 ft (81 m) below the waters of lakes, rivers, and seas. Its feet are set well back on its body, to push it through the water when it dives. On dry land, its graceful glide turns into a wobbly walk. It has a sad, yodeling call; sometimes it wails and laughs wildly. These calls sound eerie at night.

Winter

Summer

Common Loon
(Gavia immer)
Length:
3 ft (90 cm)

In winter the loon's plumage is much paler and duller than in summer.

ROSEATE SPOONBILL	ANHINGA
BELTED KINGFISHER	COMMON LOON
WHOOPING CRANE	SNAIL KITE
GREEN-BACKED HERON	

Belted Kingfisher
(Megaceryle alcyon)
Length: 13 in (33 cm)

You can tell the female by her rusty belly band below the slate blue breast band.

The stout, sharp bill is used to spear fish.

BELTED KINGFISHER

This is the only kingfisher in most of North America. It usually hovers over the water, then plunges in headfirst, to grab a fish in its strong bill. It also swoops close to the water's surface and dips down to catch a meal. It has a loud, rattling call, often made as it flies. The female lays her eggs at the end of a long tunnel in a steep bank near the water.

Great Bear Lake

Great Slave Lake

ROCKY MTS

N O R T H   A M E R I C A

PACIFIC OCEAN

St. Lawrence

Great Lakes

APPALACHIAN MTS

North American lakes, surrounded by coniferous forest, like this one on the northwest coast of Canada, are home to wading birds, such as loons and cranes.

Colorado

Rio Grande

SIERRA MADRE

Mississippi

Red

Large broad wings help the bird soar.

GULF OF MEXICO

The Everglades (see map on facing page).

	0	250	500	750 km

	0	250	500 miles

The Everglades

The tropical swamps of the Everglades in Florida, particularly the National Park in the very south of the area, are home to a unique variety of birds. Many migrating birds stop here to rest and feed too. The whole area is only just above sea level and consists of a very wide, slow-moving river covered with sedges, grasses, and rushes. There are some patches of open water and islands of trees called hummocks. Birds feed on the many insects and fish that live in this warm, humid environment.

Along the coast of the Everglades, belts of mangrove trees trap mud and silt with their roots and build up new land.

SNAIL KITE

Once called the Everglades Kite, this unusual species feeds only on water snails of the group known as apple snails, *Pomacea*. It is a treat to see this hawklike bird flapping slowly over the swamps on its large, wide wings. It has a very floppy flight. When it spots a snail, it swoops down, grabs the snail in one foot, carries it to a perch, and then eats it. Snail kites in the Everglades were once close to extinction, but they are now protected and are making a comeback.

The long, thin upper bill pulls a snail's body out of its shell.

Snail Kite
(Rostrhamus sociabilis)
Length: 18 in (46 cm)

The male has red legs; female and young have orange legs.

ROSEATE SPOONBILL

Nesting colonies of spoonbills are a spectacular sight in the Everglades. They have elaborate courtship displays, including clapping bills and giving each other twigs. To catch food, the spoonbill sweeps its sensitive bill from side to side through the water. When it feels food, such as fish, it snaps its bill shut. Spoonbills were once hunted for their feathers, which were used to decorate hats. They are now protected, and their numbers have grown.

Roseate Spoonbill
(Ajaia ajaja)
Length: 2 ft 8 in (81cm)

The broad tip of the bill is like a spoon.

It has an ear opening on the side of its head.

GREEN-BACKED HERON

The shy Green-backed Heron feeds mainly at night and likes to hide among waterside plants by day. But it has adapted well to living in urban areas near people. This wading bird grabs fish and small animals in its long, strong bill and will sometimes dive underwater to chase its prey.

The female has a tawny brown neck and breast.

ANHINGA

The Anhinga often swims on the surface with just its head and neck showing, so it looks like a snake. For this reason, it is sometimes called the snakebird. It dives deep underwater to catch fish, spearing them with its daggerlike bill. The jagged edges of its bill help the Anhinga keep a firm hold on its prey, until it can flip it up into the air and swallow it whole.

Anhinga
(Anhinga anhinga)
Length: 3 ft (91 cm)

When excited, it raises its crest.

The Green-backed Heron often crouches silent and still at the edge of water to spot its prey.

Green-backed Heron
(Butorides striatus)
Length: 19 in (48 cm)

FLORIDA EVERGLADES
GULF OF MEXICO
FLORIDA BAY
ATLANTIC OCEAN
FLORIDA KEYS

0 10 20 30 km
0 10 20 miles

Central America and the Caribbean

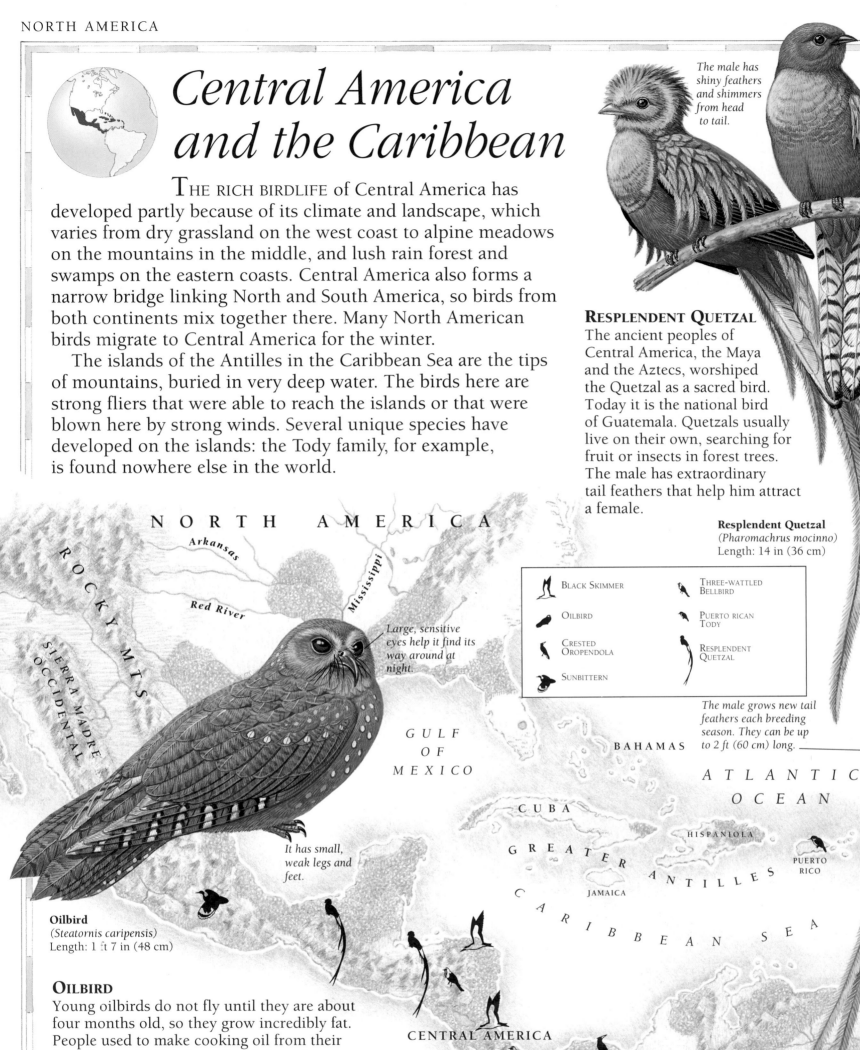

THE RICH BIRDLIFE of Central America has developed partly because of its climate and landscape, which varies from dry grassland on the west coast to alpine meadows on the mountains in the middle, and lush rain forest and swamps on the eastern coasts. Central America also forms a narrow bridge linking North and South America, so birds from both continents mix together there. Many North American birds migrate to Central America for the winter.

The islands of the Antilles in the Caribbean Sea are the tips of mountains, buried in very deep water. The birds here are strong fliers that were able to reach the islands or that were blown here by strong winds. Several unique species have developed on the islands: the Tody family, for example, is found nowhere else in the world.

The male has shiny feathers and shimmers from head to tail.

The female is dull colored and does not have a long tail.

RESPLENDENT QUETZAL

The ancient peoples of Central America, the Maya and the Aztecs, worshiped the Quetzal as a sacred bird. Today it is the national bird of Guatemala. Quetzals usually live on their own, searching for fruit or insects in forest trees. The male has extraordinary tail feathers that help him attract a female.

Resplendent Quetzal
(Pharomachrus mocinno)
Length: 14 in (36 cm)

Black Skimmer	Three-wattled Bellbird
Oilbird	Puerto rican Tody
Crested Oropendola	Resplendent Quetzal
Sunbittern	

The male grows new tail feathers each breeding season. They can be up to 2 ft (60 cm) long.

Large, sensitive eyes help it find its way around at night.

NORTH AMERICA

Arkansas
Red River
Mississippi

ROCKY MTS

SIERRA MADRE OCCIDENTAL

GULF OF MEXICO

BAHAMAS

ATLANTIC OCEAN

CUBA

HISPANIOLA

GREATER ANTILLES

PUERTO RICO

JAMAICA

CARIBBEAN SEA

LESSER ANTILLES

It has small, weak legs and feet.

Oilbird
(Steatornis caripensis)
Length: 1 ft 7 in (48 cm)

OILBIRD

Young oilbirds do not fly until they are about four months old, so they grow incredibly fat. People used to make cooking oil from their fatty flesh, which is how the bird got its name. The Oilbird lives in caves and finds its way in the darkness by making clicking sounds. These bounce back from the walls of the cave and other objects. The time it takes for the sound to bounce back helps the bird work out how far away things are. At night, it flies out of the cave to feed on oily fruits. Its good sense of smell and excellent eyesight help it find food.

CENTRAL AMERICA

GULF OF PANAMA

PACIFIC OCEAN

Orinoco

ANDES

SOUTH AMERICA

Negro

0	200	400	600 km
0		200	400 miles

Each woven nest is more than 3 ft 3 in (1 m) long and hangs from a tree branch.

The mouth opens very wide, so the bird can swallow large fruits.

Wattles hang from top of the bill and the edge of the mouth.

THREE-WATTLED BELLBIRD

Male bellbirds make probably the loudest noise of any bird. They advertise for a female by producing an explosive "bock" noise. This call can be heard 0.6 miles (1 km) away. The male displays with his mouth wide open. The female builds the nest and looks after the young. Her dull color helps camouflage her while she sits on the nest.

Three-wattled Bellbird
(Procnias tricarunculata)
Length: 12 in (30 cm)

CRESTED OROPENDOLA

Crested oropendolas live in groups and nest together too. They can build up to 100 nests in just one tree. This probably helps protect the eggs and young from enemies, as the birds can warn each other of danger. The male has a spectacular courtship display to attract a female. He makes a series of loud, gurgling sounds while flapping his wings and leaning forward so far that he almost falls off his perch.

Crested Oropendola
(Psarocolius decumanus)
Length: 17 in (43 cm)

The bird jerks its head all the time while perched.

The long straight bill snaps up insects.

Puerto Rican Tody
(Todus mexicanus)
Length: 4 in (10 cm)

PUERTO RICAN TODY

This tody lives in woods and forests. It feeds by pouncing on insects from a perch. When it flies, its wings make a whirring noise. During the breeding season, the tody uses its beak to dig tiny nesting burrows in a bank, like its relative the kingfisher. There are four other species of Caribbean tody.

SUNBITTERN

During its courtship display, the Sunbittern spreads its wings to show off the patches of orange and yellow colors on its feathers. These look like the colors of a sky at sunset, which is how the bird got its name. At other times, the mottled colors on the feathers camouflage the bird as it searches for food along stream banks in woodland areas. It catches fish, insects, and frogs, seizing its prey with its long, sharp bill.

Sunbittern
(Eurypyga helias)
Length: 18 in (46 cm)

Wings are spread out during courtship displays.

Black Skimmer
(Rynchops niger)
Length: 1 ft 8 in (50 cm)

BLACK SKIMMER

The Black Skimmer has a strange bill – the bottom part is about one-third longer than the top part. To find food, the skimmer flies over shallow water with its bill open, ploughing a furrow through the water. When its bill hits a small fish or crustacean, the skimmer snaps the top bill down like a pair of scissors to trap its prey.

Dense jungle vegetation is typical of Central America's tropical rain forests.

Amazon

Tapajós

The Amazon Rain Forest

THE AMAZON RAIN FOREST stretches from the Andes Mountains in the west to the Atlantic Ocean in the east. One-fifth of all the kinds of birds in the world live there. This is mainly because of differences in rainfall, soils, and the height of the land across the region, which provide a variety of habitats. Birds live at different layers in the trees, much as people live in apartment buildings. Each layer receives different amounts of sunlight and provides different kinds of food. Birds such as toucans and trogons live in the treetops, called the canopy. In the middle layers, live birds such as macaws and jacamars. Larger birds stalk among the fallen leaves down on the forest floor.

CUVIER'S TOUCAN

With its long bill, Cuvier's Toucan can reach out to pluck berries or seeds from trees high in the canopy. The jagged edges of its bill work like a saw to cut fruit. It also eats insects, spiders, and small birds. If its bill were as heavy as it looks, the toucan would not be able to hold up its head. Its bill is in fact hollow and extremely light. The brightly colored bill can help it recognize others of its kind.

Cuvier's Toucan
(*Ramphastos cuvieri*)
Length: 20 in (50 cm)

SCARLET MACAW

At sunrise the Scarlet Macaw flies through the forest in search of food. It squawks noisily while flying but feeds in silence. Two of its toes point forward and two point backward, so it can use its feet to grip well and hold food up to its mouth.

The macaw's powerful bill can crush the hardest seeds and nuts, but it is also used for preening and to grip branches.

COCK-OF-THE-ROCK

During courtship, the male Cock-of-the-Rock performs amazing displays on the forest floor. Up to 25 males display together, and each has his own area. They show off by leaping into the air, bobbing their heads, snapping their bills, and flicking and fanning their feathers.

Cock-of-the-Rock
(*Rupicola rupicola*)
Length: 13 in (32 cm)

Female cock-of-the-rocks are drab-colored for camouflage and look very different from the male.

Scarlet Macaw
(*Ara macao*)
Length: 2 ft 9 in (85 cm)

Short legs help the macaw keep its balance.

During his display, the male spreads his crest forward, so it almost hides his bill.

A colorful male cock-of-the-rock displays on a bare patch of forest floor called a "lek."

ATLANTIC OCEAN

Orinoco

AMAZON RAIN FOREST

Negro

Amazon

Amazon

SOUTH AMERICA

| 0 | 200 | 400 | 800 km |
| 0 | 250 | | 500 miles |

PACIFIC OCEAN

ANDES

Lake Titicaca

HARPY EAGLE		WHITE-PLUMED ANTBIRD	
WHITE-TIPPED SICKLEBILL		SCARLET MACAW	
HOATZIN		COCK-OF-THE-ROCK	
CUVIER'S TOUCAN			

Birds of the rain forest are often brightly colored, but they are hard to see against a background of leaves and patches of sunlight.

Two toes point forward and two point backward for a strong grip.

Toucans live in groups and often preen each other or play games. They wrestle with their bills or toss fruit to each other, just as we play "catch."

The Amazon is the world's largest tropical rain forest. It covers an area about three-quarters the size of the United States but is being cleared at a rapid rate.

Powerful hooked bill tears flesh from food.

Harpy Eagle
(Harpia harpyja)
Length: 3 ft 7 in
(1.10 m)

Massive sharp talons enable the eagle to grab and crush prey.

The Harpy Eagle pursues capuchin monkeys and other small animals, such as opossums and coatis, through the rain forest.

HARPY EAGLE
The huge and fearsome Harpy Eagle swoops through the treetops seeking its prey. It can fly at speeds of up to 80 kph (50 mph). Its gray, mottled coloring helps camouflage it among the leaves, so the animals it hunts do not see it coming. A pair of Harpy Eagles builds a nest of sticks high up in the trees.

Like all hummers, sicklebills hover around vegetation.

WHITE-TIPPED SICKLEBILL
The sicklebill is a hummingbird. Hummingbirds are so named because of the sound made by their wings, which flap at more than 100 beats per second. The long curved bill of the sicklebill probes the sweet nectar inside flowers. The tongue forms a tube like a straw, through which it can suck up nectar. Nectar is easy to digest; it provides instant energy to power the hummingbird's whirring wings; it also helps keep the bird warm.

White-tipped Sicklebill
(Eutoxeres aquila)
Length: 5 in (13 cm)

White-plumed Antbird
(Pithys albifrons)
Length: 4 in (11 cm)

WHITE-PLUMED ANTBIRD
Despite its name, the White-plumed Antbird does not eat ants. It feeds on spiders and insects that are trying to escape from army ants. Usually, the antbird darts down to the ground or hangs from a branch to snatch up a meal. But sometimes it will hop among the ants, holding its tail up out of the way. Its long legs help protect it from the ants' stings.

The antbird often perches on a small tree and waits for ants to appear.

Hoatzin
(Opisthocomus hoazin)
Length: 2 ft 2 in (66 cm)

HOATZIN
Using its weak wings, the Hoatzin flaps clumsily through flooded areas of the rain forest along quiet riverbanks. It uses its wings and tail to help it clamber through the trees, as its feet are not very strong. Hoatzins move about and nest in groups, building untidy twig nests by the water. Young hoatzins leave the nest soon after hatching and may leap into the water to escape danger.

Columns of army ants swarm over the forest floor.

A baby Hoatzin has two tiny claws on the bend of each wing, to help it grip and climb.

The Andes

THE ANDES ARE THE world's longest mountain chain, stretching down the entire western coast of South America. The steep slopes act as a barrier to birds, so that species on the east side of the mountains differ from those on the west. Plant-life in the Andes also varies dramatically over short distances, creating a variety of habitats. These range from rainforests on the lower slopes, through drier forests and grass plains higher up, to frozen wilderness near the peaks. On the upper slopes, it is so cold that some hummingbirds go into semi-hibernation at night – they slow down all their body processes and lower their body temperature, so they use less energy.

TORRENT DUCK

The fast-flowing rivers and streams of the Andes are home to the Torrent Duck. Its sharp claws and powerful legs help it cling to slippery rocks; the stiff tail is useful for balancing and steering the duck when in water. It dives underwater to catch food, such as insects, but it also picks up food floating by on the surface. Ducklings are able to swim with their parents as soon as they hatch.

The body is streamlined to help the duck swim fast.

Torrent Duck
(*Merganetta armata*)
Length: 18 in (46 cm)

ANDEAN CONDOR

This huge vulture is the world's heaviest bird of prey, weighing up to 31 lb (14 kg). The Andean Condor soars for long distances on outstretched wings, sometimes rising to heights of 23,000 ft (7,000 m) in the mountains. It has very keen eyesight and can spot dead animals to feed on, from high up in the sky. It will also kill sick or wounded animals. Some Andean condors raid seabird colonies on the coast and take the eggs and chicks.

The condor probably has the greatest wingspan of any landbird.

The bare head enables the bird to reach into a carcass without getting its feathers dirty.

Andean Condor
(*Vultur gryphus*)
Length: 3 ft 4 in (1.1 m)
Wingspan: up to 10 ft (3 m)

SWORD-BILLED HUMMINGBIRD

This bird's extraordinary bill enables it to reach nectar and insects deep inside trumpet-shaped flowers. The hummingbird hovers below the flowers to feed. As it does so, pollen is caught on its feathers. The bird then carries this to other flowers, pollinating the plants (helping them to produce seeds). More than half the flowers in the Andes are pollinated by hummingbirds instead of insects.

Sword-billed Hummingbird
(*Ensifera ensifera*)
Length: 3 in (7.5 cm)
Length of bill: 4 in (10.5 cm)

The long bill for reaches pollen inside fuchsias and other trumpet-shaped flowers.

0 250 500 750 km
0 250 500 miles

Areas of dense rain forest shrouded in mist cover the lower slopes of the Andes.

CARIBBEAN SEA

SOUTH AMERICA

ANDES

Negro
Amazon
Madeira
Japurá
Marañón
Ucayali
São Francisco

GREATER RHEA

The Greater Rhea is very much like the African Ostrich, except that it has three toes on each foot, instead of two. It cannot fly, but it can sprint faster than a horse, reaching speeds of 31 mph (50 kph). During the breeding season, males fight for territory and for females. Several females lay their eggs in one male's nest.

Rheas have three strong toes with claws on each foot for defense and for great speed.

Long legs make it easy to run swiftly, when necessary.

Common Caracara
(Polyborus plancus)
Length: 2 ft (60 cm)

BURROWING OWL

Unlike most owls, burrowing owls are often active during the day. They usually live in abandoned mud burrows of other animals and spend a lot of time perched at the entrance like sentinels. If disturbed, they bob up and down and make a chattering noise. Burrowing owls can run quickly over the grasslands on their long legs to catch their food – usually insects; they also dine on small reptiles.

Greater Rhea
(Rhea americana)
Length: 5 ft (1.5 m)
Height: 4 ft 3 in (1.3 m)

COMMON CARACARA

These chicken-sized birds of prey are related to falcons. Caracaras build their own nests, unlike true falcons, which use abandoned nests. They eat a varied diet, from small mammals, birds, fish, and frogs to insects and dead meat – they often join vultures to feed on a carcass. Caracaras are rather slow and lazy birds, but they have long legs and can move quickly if in danger.

This owl nests in burrows made by viscachas and other animals, but it can also dig its own burrow.

Burrowing Owl
(Athene cunicularia)
Length: 10 in (25 cm)

The Pampas

THE GRASSY PLAINS of the pampas lie in the southeastern corner of South America. The climate is generally dry, with hot summers and cool winters. In the dry season, lightning can cause fires; farmers also set light to the grass, to encourage new shoots to grow. Many birds nest under the ground, where they are safer from fires and people. Large cattle ranches on the pampas have damaged the natural environment. Only birds that can adapt to human disturbance, such as ovenbirds, have survived. Others have died out or decreased in number. Huge flocks of rheas are no longer common.

Paraná

Uruguay

Paraná

P A M P A S

Lake Titicaca

A N D E S

PACIFIC OCEAN

The vast, treeless plains of the pampas provide little shelter for birds, so they nest by rocks or under the ground.

RUFOUS HORNERO

The mud nest of the Rufous Hornero looks rather like an old fashioned baker's oven, so these birds are sometimes called ovenbirds. (The word *hornero* means "baker" in Spanish.) It takes the bird months to build one nest, which is about twice the size of a soccer ball, yet it starts a new one each year. The Rufous Hornero strides across open ground on its long legs, lifting its feet high in the air. It uses its strong, sharp bill to dig up worms and insect larvae.

Rufous Hornero
(Furnarius rufus)
Length: 7 in (19 cm)

The nest is made of thousands of lumps of mud, reinforced with straw, and baked hard in the hot sun.

The Galapagos Islands

ISLA MARCHENA

On this flat island, the back of a giant tortoise makes a good look-out post for a passing Galapagos hawk.

THE LONELY GALAPAGOS ISLANDS, which lie in the Pacific Ocean, west of Ecuador, are like nowhere else on Earth. The islands are the tops of huge volcanoes that rose up from the seabed millions of years ago. An extraordinary variety of birds live among the dry cactus scrub and jagged volcanic rocks. Many of them are found only on these islands. There are two main reasons that the birdlife of the Galapagos Islands is so unique. First, the islands are so far from the mainland of South America that only a few birds have managed to reach them. These were able to develop into a variety of species because there was little competition for food and nesting places. Second, the warm waters from the Pacific and cool waters from the Antarctic flow past the islands. This means that birds usually found in cold places, such as penguins and albatrosses, live side by side with tropical species, such as flamingos and frigatebirds.

GALAPAGOS ISLANDS

ISLA SAN SALVADOR

ISLA FERNANDINA

The frigatebird has the greatest wingspan of any bird, in relation to the size of its body.

The tiny wings are only 10 in (25 cm) long.

ISLA ISABELA

PACIFIC OCEAN

Flightless Cormorant
(Nannopterum harrisi)
Length: 3 ft 1 in (95 cm)

DARWIN'S FINCHES

The 13 different species of Galapagos finch look similar because they probably originated from one species. But each species has a different-shaped bill designed to get at a different food. In studying these birds, the British naturalist Charles Darwin worked out his theory of evolution. This explains how plants and animals may have changed over many generations to suit their habitat.

Charles Darwin
1809-1882

Warbler Finch (Certhidea olivacea)
This finch has a fine, pointed bill to catch small insects.

Tree Finch (Camarhynchus parvulus)
This insectivorous tree finch has a thicker bill to cope with fruit, buds, small seeds, and insects.

Ground Finch
(Geospiza magnirostris)
This large ground finch has a heavy, strong bill for crushing seeds.

Woodpecker Finch
(Camarhynchus parvulus)
This is one of the few birds to use a twig as a tool. It uses the twig to find insect grubs under bark and tease them out.

It nests on rocks close to the sea.

FLIGHTLESS CORMORANT

The Flightless Cormorant uses its small, ragged wings to balance on land and shade its chick from the hot sun. But its wings are too weak for flying or swimming. It probably lost its powers of flight because there were originally no enemies to fly away from, and it was able to get all its food close to the shore. This made it easy for people to hunt, and it became rare. Now it is protected. It is the only remaining cormorant that cannot fly.

GALAPAGOS PENGUIN

This rare penguin is able to live so near the Equator because of the cool waters of the Humboldt Current, which flow past the Galapagos Islands. It feeds on fish and nests in small groups, laying its eggs in nests of stones, caves, or holes. Like all penguins, this one is well adapted for fast swimming underwater. It has flippers like fins, webbed feet, and a streamlined body shape. But it is clumsy on land. It hops shakily from one rock to another, holding out its little flippers for balance. When it reaches the water, it jumps in feet first.

Strong flippers help the penguin "fly" underwater.

Galapagos Penguin
(Spheniscus mendiculus)
Length: 1 ft 8 in (51 cm)

MAGNIFICENT FRIGATEBIRD

The frigatebird soars over the islands on its huge wings. It feeds on turtles, jellyfish, and seabird chicks and can skim across the sea, lifting out fish with its hooked bill. It also chases other birds, such as boobies, to make them drop the food they are carrying. It then twists and turns, snatching the food in mid-air. It is named after the pirate ships called frigates, because it steals from others rather like a pirate. To attract a mate, the male frigatebird puffs out his red throat.

Magnificent Frigatebird
(*Fregata magnificens*)
Length: 3 ft 6 in (1.1 m)
Wingspan: up to
7 ft 9 in (2.4 m)

GALAPAGOS DOVE

During courtship, the male Galapagos dove struts around the female, bowing, spreading his tail, and letting his wings droop. He puffs up his feathers to make himself look bigger and more important. The female dove lays her eggs in a rough nest of grass, usually built under a rock.

Male

Galapagos Dove
(*Zenaida galapagoensis*)
Length: 8 in (20 cm)

Female

With its powerful bill pointing straight up to the sky during courtship, the bird "moos" like a cow.

WAVED ALBATROSS

This bird, also known as the Galapagos Albatross, nests only on the volcanic cliffs on the island of Española. No one knows why. Like all albatrosses, waved albatrosses have an elaborate courtship dance. A male and female face each other and go through a variety of set movements, such as clapping the lower bill up and down, touching sides, pointing the bills to the sky, and one bird circling its bill around its partner's bill. The clapping noise they make is very loud and sounds like a football rattle.

Waved Albatross
(*Diomedea irrorata*)
Length: 3 ft (94 cm)

ISLA SANTA CRUZ

ISLA SAN CRISTOBAL

ISLA ESPAÑOLA

FLIGHTLESS CORMORANT
WAVED ALBATROSS
GALAPAGOS PENGUIN
GALAPAGOS DOVE
BLUE-FOOTED BOOBY
MAGNIFICENT FRIGATEBIRD
CACTUS FINCH
WOODPECKER FINCH
TREE FINCH
GROUND FINCH

ISLA SANTA MARIA

0   10   20   30 km
0   10   20 miles

The long, jagged bill is designed to catch fish underwater.

Blue-footed Booby
(*Sula nebouxii*)
Length: 2 ft 10 in (86 cm)

To impress their partners, these boobies parade up and down, lifting and spreading their bright blue feet.

The Galapagos Islands were formed by volcanoes erupting in the Pacific Ocean, so much of the landscape consists of black volcanic rock.

BLUE-FOOTED BOOBY

These birds nest in small scattered colonies. Unlike other boobies, they feed close to the shore. This means that the different species of booby do not compete with each other. Because they have a good food supply nearby, blue-footed boobies can raise two or three young each year. Other species have only one chick. The young boobies are fed on fish coughed up by their parents. The booby's strange name comes from the Spanish word *bobo*, which means "clown."

Europe

THE SMALL CONTINENT of Europe has been covered with ice at least four times in the past million years. In fact, the climate in northern Europe is still very cold. The generally cold climate means that many birds are forced to migrate south for the winter.

Europe does not have a huge variety of bird species, partly due to the cold climate in the north, but also because of the large numbers of people who live there – many more than in North America. People have cleared away the forests, polluted the land and water, and hunted the birds. Birds that cannot live in cities, parks, or gardens have been driven to remote areas, such as mountains, moors, and marshes.

Many coastal habitats in Europe are, however, very rich in birdlife. Estuaries provide vital feeding and resting areas for water birds and waders migrating south from the Arctic. Sea cliffs are home to spectacular nesting colonies of seabirds, such as gannets, guillemots, puffins, and razorbills.

EUROPE UNDER ICE

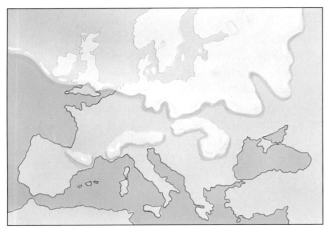

This map shows the extent of the ice sheet 11, 000 years ago – at the end of Europe's last ice age.

At various times in the Earth's history, there have been cold spells called ice ages, which have lasted thousands of years. During an ice age, ice sheets and glaciers spread across the Earth's surface. Over the past 900,000 years, there have been about 10 major ice ages. At the height of the last ice age, about 18,000 years ago, great ice sheets spread out from the North Pole, covering much of Europe. Some birds died out, while others moved south to warmer places. About 10,000 years ago, the climate became warmer again, the ice receded, and some of the birds returned to the north.

CLIMATE AND LANDSCAPE

The climate of Europe ranges from the cold, rainy, and snowy northern lands, such as the British Isles and Scandinavia, to the hot, dry Mediterranean lands of the south, such as Italy and Greece. In the middle are warm, wet areas that have a mild climate. A warm ocean current called the Gulf Stream flows from the Caribbean past the western shores of Europe, making the winter climate on the west coast less severe. Europe's landscape includes long mountain chains, such as the Alps and the Pyrenees, which stop birds from moving freely from north to south.

AMAZING BIRDS OF EUROPE

Goldcrest
(Regulus regulus)

Smallest bird
The tiny Goldcrest is the smallest European bird.

Fastest bird
The Peregrine Falcon is the fastest bird in the world. It reaches speeds of up to 112 mph (180 kph) when swooping down to chase its prey.

Longest legs
The Black-winged Stilt has the longest legs, in relation to the length of its body, of any bird. It can feed in very deep water.

Varied eggs
The Guillemot has a greater variety of colors and patterns on its eggs than that of any other bird. This means the parents can recognize their own eggs on the crowded cliff ledges where they nest.

Largest clutch
The female Gray Partridge lays the most eggs at one time of any bird – as many as 15-19 eggs in one clutch. She lays so many because a large proportion of the chicks do not survive.

Marvelous mimic
The Marsh Warbler is the world champion bird mimic. It can copy the songs of about 76 other bird species.

Greatest stamina
The Swift spends more time in the air than any other land bird does. It sleeps, eats, and drinks on the wing for up to three years, at heights of up to 6,500 ft (2,000 m).

Swift
(Apus apus)

Many people live and farm in the sunny Mediterranean region, growing trees such as these olives. This means there are fewer places for birds to live.

FACTS ABOUT EUROPE

Longest coastline
Europe has a longer coastline in proportion to its size than that of any other continent. Norway's coastline is indented with steep valleys called fjords (above) that were cut into the cliffs by thick glaciers during the last ice age.

Number of birds
More than 600 species of bird have been spotted in Europe. Of these, about 430 birds are regularly seen there.

Longest glacier
The longest glacier in the Alps is called the Aletsch; it is more than 15 miles (24 km) long.

High population
Europe occupies only about 7 percent of the world's land area, yet 14 percent of the world's population – about 690 million people – live there.

Main mountain
Mont Blanc is 15,770 ft (4,807 m) tall and is western Europe's highest mountain. It forms part of the Alps mountain range, which stretches for 660 miles (1,100 km).

Volcanic eruptions
The only active volcano on mainland Europe is Vesuvius, in Italy. It began erupting 10,000 years ago and buried the towns of Pompeii and Stabiae in AD 79.

Longest rivers
The longest rivers in Europe are the Volga – 2,194 miles (3,531 km); the Danube – 1,776 miles (2,858 km); and the Dnieper – 1,420 miles (2,285 km).

Largest sea
Europe's Mediterranean Sea is the largest sea in the world.

TYPICAL BIRDS

Here are a few examples of typical birds from the most important habitats of Europe. These range from dark conifer forests in the north to more open broad-leaved woodlands farther south and dry scrubland around the shores of the Mediterranean. Rivers, lakes, marshes, and coasts are also major European bird habitats. You can find out more on the next few pages.

Moorland
Birds such as this Merlin nest on European moors in summer. They move to marshlands and shores in winter, where more food is available.

Mountains
Mountains provide refuges from towns and farms for birds such as this Chough, as well as for golden eagles, and vultures.

Coasts
Seabirds such as this Puffin, along with guillemots, gulls, gannets, and terns, nest in densely packed colonies. They can be found on cliffs, beaches, and islands around the coasts of Europe in spring and summer.

Mediterranean scrub
The rich variety of insects in the Mediterranean scrublands in summer attract insect-eating birds, such as this Hoopoe, along with rollers, shrikes, and honey buzzards. Many migrate south to Africa in winter.

Towns and cities
Birds such as this Rock Dove (the common pigeon), as well as starlings, sparrows, and kestrels, have made themselves at home in urban habitats. Pigeons nest on the window ledges of tall buildings as if the ledges, with their nooks and crannies, were cliffs by the coast.

Estuaries and shores
In winter, waders such as this Redshank, along with godwits, dunlins, and curlews, gather in flocks on estuaries and shores to feed on creatures in the mud and sand.

Forests and woodlands
Warblers such as this Wood Warbler, along with thrushes, jays, woodpeckers, owls, and tits, are common in the remaining areas of European forests and woodlands.

EUROPE

CARPATHIAN MTS

Dnieper

Don

URAL MTS

Danube

BLACK SEA

Volga

CAUCASUS MTS

CASPIAN SEA

ARAL SEA

ASIA

CYPRUS

Tigris

Euphrates

MEDITERRANEAN SEA

Forests and Woodlands

FROM THE EVERGREEN forests of the north to the broad-leaved woodland areas farther south, European forests provide a rich habitat for birds. Tree trunks and branches are safe nesting places; nuts and berries on the trees, as well as the numerous insects that live on them, provide ample food. The northern forests are generally darker and colder than those farther south, which have a greater variety of food and nesting places. Unfortunately, many of Europe's forests are now threatened. Large areas have been cleared to make way for houses or farms, and other regions have been polluted by poisonous chemicals emitted from vehicles and factories.

European forest and woodland birds have to arrange their lives around the seasons. In spring and summer, they nest and rear their young; in autumn, they eat as much as possible to build up stores of fat in their bodies; and in winter, they may fly south to warmer places or roam widely through the forest in search of food.

JAY

The harsh, screeching call of Jays can often be heard in broad-leaved woodlands, especially in spring, when they chase each other noisily through the trees as part of their courtship display. Jays feed on acorns, which they often carry for long distances, and then bury to eat during the cold winter months. Acorns that are not eaten grow into new oak trees, helping the woodlands spread. Jays also eat other nuts, berries, worms, spiders, and the eggs and young of other birds.

The crest is often raised, making the bird's head look square-shaped.

Jay
(*Garrulus glandarius*)
Length: 13 in (33 cm)

NORTHERN SPARROWHAWK

The agile, fast-flying sparrowhawk makes swift surprise attacks on blue tits and other small birds. They have little chance of escaping its needle-sharp talons. Before eating its prey, the sparrowhawk plucks off the bird's feathers. The female tears up food that the male has caught, to feed to the young.

The female is larger than the male and has gray bars underneath.

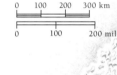
Blue tits

Short, rounded wings allow the bird to twist and turn through trees.

Northern Sparrowhawk
(*Accipiter nisus*)
Length: up to 15 in (38 cm)

Crossbills nest and feed high in the tree-tops of coniferous forests. They pull seeds from pine cones and rarely venture down to the forest floor.

GREAT GRAY OWL		NORTHERN SPARROWHAWK
WAXWING		JAY
GREEN WOODPECKER		LONG-TAILED TIT
CAPERCAILLIE		

The tail is longer than the body – no other woodland bird has such a long tail.

LONG-TAILED TIT
The tiny, restless Long-tailed Tit flits about in flocks, feeding on insects, spiders, and seeds. In spring, it builds an elaborate nest of moss, cobwebs, and hair, lined with thousands of feathers to keep its young warm. The nest is so small that adult birds have to fold their tails over their heads to fit inside it.

Long-tailed Tit
(Aegithalos caudatus)
Length: 6 in (14 cm)

Large circles of feathers on face collect sounds rather like radar dishes.

GREAT GRAY OWL
The incredibly sharp hearing of this huge owl means that it can hunt voles. Even in winter, it can hear them run through tunnels beneath deep snow. The Great Gray Owl defends its nest fiercely and will sometimes strike people, if they get too close. The owlets leave the nest when they are 3-4 weeks old but take a week or so longer to learn how to fly.

Great Gray Owl
(Strix nebulosa)
Length: up to 2 ft 7 in (84 cm)
Wingspan: over 5 ft (1.5 m)

The male Capercaillie fans out his tail, points his bill in the air, and puffs out his throat feathers during his courtship display.

Lake Onega

Volga

Capercaillie
(Tetrao urogallus)
Length: male 2 ft 10in (84 cm); female 2 ft (60 cm)

Enormous pine trees are typical of the coniferous forests of northern Europe, particularly in Scandinavia.

Comblike fringes on its toes may help the bird walk on snow without sinking in.

CAPERCAILLIE
This bird lives in conifer forests, feeding on pine seeds and needles in winter and leaves, stems, and berries in summer. It nests on the forest floor. During his courtship display, the male challenges rival males with an extraordinary song, which ends with a popping and gurgling sound – like a cork being pulled out of a bottle and the drink being poured.

There are tiny red waxlike blobs on the wings.

Waxwing
(Bombycilla garrulus)
Length: 7 in (18 cm)

Male has black and red "moustache"; female's moustache is all black.

GREEN WOODPECKER
This woodpecker is sometimes called the "yaffle," after its loud, laughing call. It has a large, dagger-like bill for probing ant hills or boring into tree trunks, and a very long tongue for licking up the insects hidden inside. It lives mainly on insects but also eats fruit and seeds. During courtship, pairs of green wood-peckers spiral around trees.

Green Woodpecker
(Picus viridis)
Length: 13 in (33 cm)

Green woodpeckers spend a lot of time on the ground, searching for ants.

Rowan berries are a favorite food.

WAXWING
The red tips on some of this bird's wing feathers look like sealing wax, which explains why it is called a Waxwing. The Waxwing likes to live in groups and chatters loudly during the breeding season. During courtship, male and female birds pass food from bill to bill. Food is mainly fruit and berries from trees and shrubs.

29

The Mediterranean

IN SOUTHERN EUROPE and around the shores of the Mediterranean Sea, the climate is warmer and drier than it is farther north. People have cleared away most of the forests that originally grew here, leaving small evergreen trees, thorny shrubs, heathers, and scented herbs in their place. During the long, hot summers, the air is alive with buzzing insects, which provide a rich food supply for warblers, bee-eaters, rollers, and other insect-eating birds. Large numbers of birds, such as storks, buzzards, and eagles, pass through the Mediterranean region as they migrate between Europe and Africa. The area also has some important marshland nature reserves, in particular, the Camargue in France and the Coto de Doñana in southern Spain.

The roller swoops down from a perch to catch insects.

The lagoons of the Coto de Doñana nature reserve attract large numbers of water birds. The reserve has the largest heron colony in Europe.

European Roller
(Coracias garrulus)
Length: 12 in (30 cm)

EUROPEAN ROLLER

All rollers are named after the male's rolling display flight: he flies up high, then dives down, rocking from side to side and somersaulting through the air. The European Roller eats mainly insects, but also hunts for lizards, snails, frogs, and other birds. In autumn it migrates south to Africa.

HOOPOE

The Hoopoe is named after its loud call, which sounds like "hoo-poo-poo." It walks and runs over the ground, searching for worms and insects with its thin, curved bill. If a bird of prey flies overhead, the adult Hoopoe spreads its wings and tail flat against the ground and points its bill straight up, ready to attack the enemy. When it is excited, it raises the crest on its head.

Golden Oriole
(Oriolus oriolus)
Length: 10 in (25 cm)

The male is brightly colored, to attract the paler female.

GOLDEN ORIOLE

The woven grassy nest of the Golden Oriole hangs below a forked branch like a hammock. It is a shy bird that spends most of its time hidden high in the treetops, feeding on insects and fruit. The female grasps food in her sharp, stout bill, to feed to her young. The Golden Oriole flies swiftly. During courtship, the male flies after the female in a high-speed chase.

The female does most of the nest building and takes care of the young.

Hoopoe
(Upupa epops)
Length: 11 in (28 cm)

The Hoopoe flaps its rounded black and white wings, rather like a butterfly.

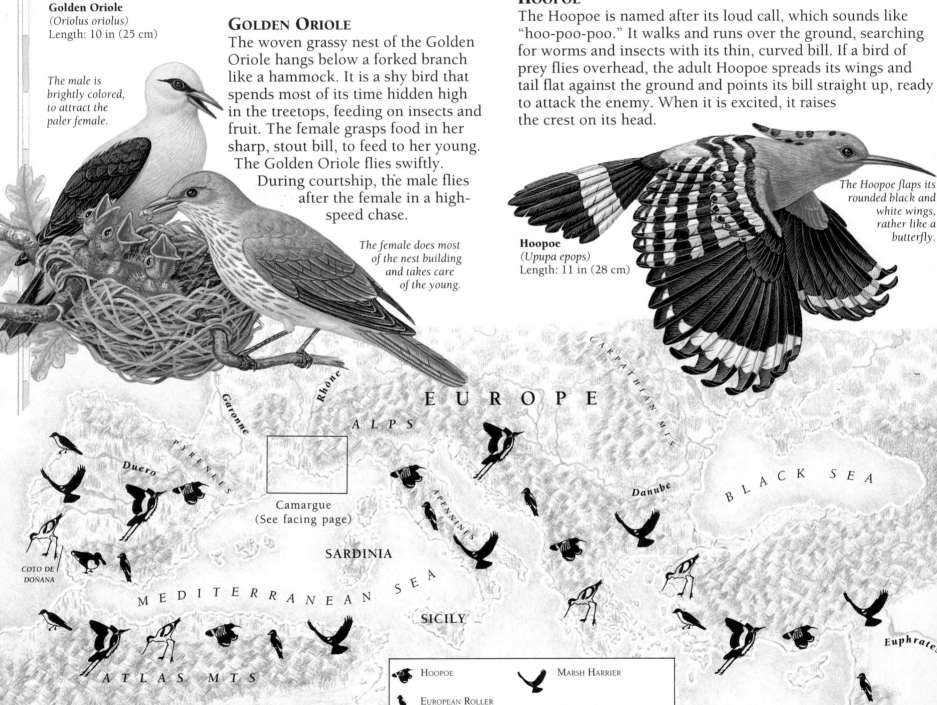

Camargue
(See facing page)

EUROPE

ALPS

Rhône

Garonne

Duero

PYRENEES

CARPATHIAN MTS

Danube

BLACK SEA

APENNINES

SARDINIA

COTO DE DOÑANA

MEDITERRANEAN SEA

SICILY

Euphrates

ATLAS MTS

NORTH AFRICA

HOOPOE		MARSH HARRIER	
EUROPEAN ROLLER		GOLDEN ORIOLE	
NORTHERN SHOVELER		PURPLE HERON	
PIED AVOCET			

0   250   500 km

0   150   300 miles

The Camargue

The salty marshes and shallow lakes of the Camargue nature reserve formed where the River Rhône meets the Mediterranean Sea. Despite the disturbance of people, houses, and industry all around and aircraft flying overhead, large numbers of wading birds and water birds live there; still more pass through on their migration routes. Tens of thousands of swans, ducks, and geese visit the Camargue in winter from their breeding grounds in northern Europe and Siberia. The birds share the available food by feeding in different places and on different types of food: stilts feed in shallow water, while little egrets and purple herons prefer deeper water; herons catch fish, while flamingos and avocets feed on small water creatures.

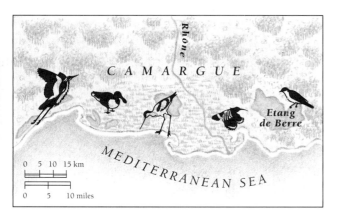

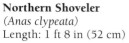

Marsh Harrier
(Circus aeruginosus)
Length: up to 1 ft 10 in (56 cm)

With wings held in a shallow V shape, it glides and soars over marshes.

MARSH HARRIER

As it glides and flaps slowly over reed beds and grassland, the male Marsh Harrier searches for frogs, fish, small mammals, birds, and insects to eat. The female and her young stay on the nest, hidden among reeds and marsh plants. When the male approaches the nest, he drops the food and the female flies up and catches it in mid-air. They also pass food like this during courtship.

Females are brown; adult males are gray. You see many more females than males.

The very sharp, pointed bill is used for grabbing fish and frogs.

Purple Heron
(Ardea purpurea)
Length: up to 3 ft (90 cm)

PURPLE HERON

The tall, slender Purple Heron has long toes to spread out its weight so that it can stalk over floating marsh plants easily, without sinking in. Its long legs allow it to wade into deep water, where it fishes for food with its long, dagger-like bill. The purple heron usually nests in small groups of up to 20 pairs. The nests are hidden among reeds or rushes growing in shallow water. It is about six weeks before the young are able to fly away from the nest. When alarmed, the Purple Heron crouches with its bill pointing straight up. This pose, along with the stripes on its neck, make it hard to see among the reeds.

The heron is a shy bird, which it is hard to see until it takes off, usually making a squawking noise.

Greater flamingos feed on plants and small animals in the shallow waters of the Camargue. Three-quarters of all the flamingo chicks in the Mediterranean region hatch here.

PIED AVOCET

The pointed upturned bill of the pied avocet sweeps through water, or the soft mud beneath it, in search of food, such as worms and small water creatures. Avocets prefer to nest on islands, where their young are safer from attack. They usually nest in large colonies, so they can join forces against enemies.

Northern Shoveler
(Anas clypeata)
Length: 1 ft 8 in (52 cm)

The male is more colorful than the female.

Male

The big, spadelike bill filters food from water.

Pied Avocet
(Recurvirostra avosetta)
Length: 17 in (43 cm)

The bird has long legs and a long bill, so that it can feed in deep water.

NORTHERN SHOVELER

This bird gets its name from its shovel-shaped bill. At first, the chick has a normal bill, but this shape alters as it grows up. The adult shoveler sucks water into its wide bill and then pushes it out of the sides. Fine "combs" on the inside edges of the bill trap floating animals and plants from the water, as it flows over them.

Coastal Areas

EUROPE'S JAGGED, IRREGULAR coastline provides many nesting places for seabirds. Millions come ashore in summer to lay their eggs and raise their young on cliff ledges, beaches, and islands. Sea breezes along the coast help with takeoff and landing. Although steep cliffs are dangerous for young birds, it is harder for enemies to reach them. There is also safety in numbers. Many seabirds crowd together in huge, noisy, smelly colonies made up of thousands of birds. Different species, such as guillemots, kittiwakes, gannets, and fulmars, may nest together on the same cliff. Each species nests at a different level. In this way, they share the small amount of space available. Unlike land birds, seabirds do not need a large feeding area or territory on land to gather food for their chicks. They feed mainly out at sea, so they can nest close together on land.

Large, powerful wings are useful for gliding and soaring.

Long, strong legs are equipped for running and webbed feet for swimming.

Great Black-backed Gull
(Larus marinus)
Length: up to 31 in (79 cm)

GREAT BLACK-BACKED GULL
This large gull is a fierce hunter, taking a wide variety of prey, from fish and seabirds to rabbits. In the summer breeding season, it attacks seabird colonies on the coast, gulping down a chick in a single mouthful. At other times of year, it scavenges for scraps on rubbish heaps inland and around fishing ports and beaches.

LITTLE TERN
Bustling colonies of little terns gather on sandy beaches in summer. Members of the colony may help each other dive-bomb enemies and drive them away. Young terns have to learn the best places to fish and how to dive headfirst into the water like their parents. At first, their dives may be more like belly flops, but they soon learn. Sadly, the numbers of these terns have decreased because of people disturbing them.

The shallow seas along Europe's coasts are rich in food for the vast colonies of seabirds that nest there in summer.

Long, pointed wings beat quickly up and down.

It has a graceful and agile flight, sometimes hovering over the water.

Little Tern
(Sterna albifrons)
Length: 9 in (23 cm)

The sharp, pointed bill is used to grip fish.

GUILLEMOT
The Guillemot, or Common Murre, spends a lot of time far out at sea. To catch fish, it dives below the surface, beats its wings rapidly, and steers with its feet. It comes to the coasts only to breed, forming dense colonies on cliff ledges. The birds are usually packed so close together that they touch their neighbors. This Guillemot lays a single egg on a bare, rocky cliff ledge (other guillemots lay two eggs). It does not build a nest, so one parent always has to stay and protect the egg and chick.

STORM PETREL
The Storm Petrel is the smallest European seabird. Fluttering above the water like a bat, it picks up small fish and plankton from the surface. A Storm Petrel will often follow ships to feed on the scraps thrown overboard; it may shelter near ships during storms. It nests in colonies, mostly on isolated islands because it cannot defend itself easily.

The streamlined shape helps the bird move fast through water.

Guillemot
(Uria aalge)
Length: 16 in (41 cm)

As it feeds, the bird's legs dangle down – it looks as if it is "walking" on water.

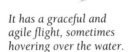
Narrow, pointed bill is equipped to seize fish.

The bill is slim and hooked.

Storm Petrel
(Hydrobates pelagicus)
Length: 6 in (15 cm)

MANX SHEARWATER

On dark nights, the wails and screams of shearwaters returning to their nesting burrows sound spooky. They gather in huge groups, called "rafts," near the coast, waiting for darkness before coming in to land. This helps them avoid enemy attack.

Stiff, straight wings allow it to glide close to the water.

Manx Shearwater
(Puffinus puffinus)
Length: 15 in (38 cm)

BALTIC SEA

NORTH SEA

BRITISH ISLES

Elbe

ENGLISH CHANNEL

Rhine

ATLANTIC OCEAN

Loire

Garonne

Duero

Gannets breed in vast colonies of more than 200,000 pairs. They usually remain faithful to one partner.

EUROPE

APENNINES

CORSICA

SARDINIA

MEDITERRANEAN SEA

SICILY

SAFETY IN NUMBERS

More than 95 percent of the world's seabirds, such as these puffins, nest in colonies of thousands of birds. This gives their eggs and young a good chance of surviving. Enemies are less likely to attack a colony, where they have to face large numbers of birds at once. The birds also warn each other of approaching danger. Some birds that nest in groups fly off the nest to attack an enemy. Others sit on their nests and make a lot of fuss and noise to drive attackers away.

Atlantic Puffin
(Fratercula arctica)
Length: 12 in (32 cm)

Sharp edges to the top bill and spines on the tongue help hold up to 50 small fish at a time.

The webbed feet spread out like brakes to slow the puffin down, as it comes in to land.

Northern Gannet
(Sula bassana)
Length: 3 ft (90 cm)

Streamlined body shape enables gannets to dive like torpedoes into the sea from great heights.

NORTHERN GANNET

To catch fish, the gannet makes spectacular dives into the sea. Its strong skull helps it withstand the impact of hitting the water, and its nostrils are closed off underwater. It uses its stout bill to drag prey, such as fish and squid, to the surface. In the breeding season, gannets nest very close together. After about 14 weeks, the chicks head out to sea. They do not develop their adult colors for five to six years.

ATLANTIC PUFFIN

The puffin feeds on fish that it catches underwater. It has webbed feet and small wings, which it uses to propel itself through the water. During the breeding season, the puffin develops a larger, more powerful bill to attract a mate. The bill is also used to dig a nesting burrow in a grassy clifftop. When it has grown its feathers, the young puffin leaves its burrow under cover of darkness to avoid enemies.

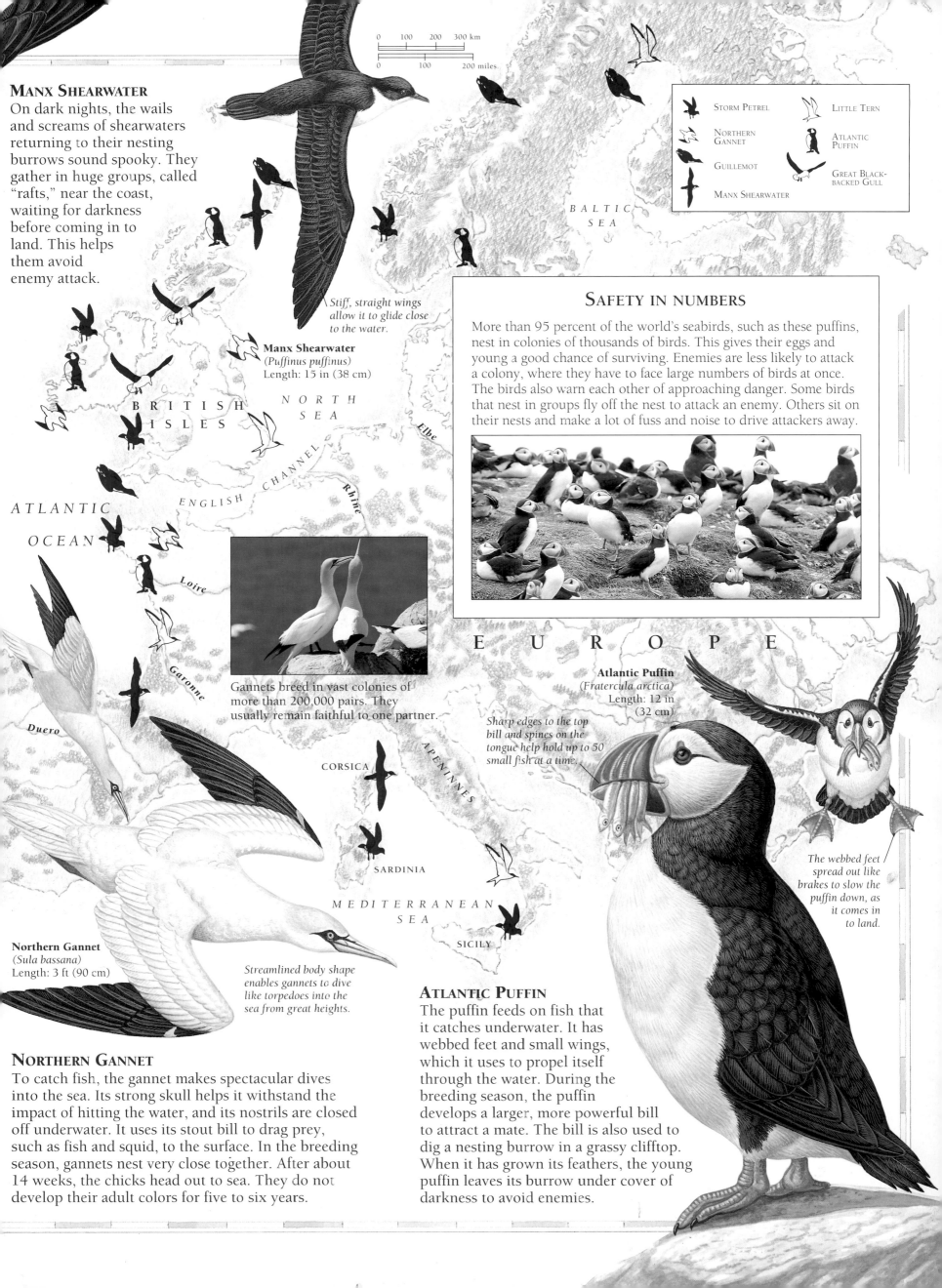

Africa

AFRICA IS THE SECOND LARGEST continent in the world. It is nearly three times the size of Europe, but about the same number of people live there. It was cut off from the other continents for millions of years, and many of its birds – the Ostrich, the Shoebill, the Secretary Bird, as well as turacos, mousebirds, wood hoopoes, and helmet shrikes – are not found anywhere else in the world.

Africa is mainly a dry continent with large areas of desert and dry grassland. As a result, it has many land birds, especially seed-eaters.

The vast Sahara Desert forms a barrier to birds flying south across Africa, although millions of birds do make this journey every year to escape the European winter. The desert is spreading because of climate change and increased periods of drought. People have also caused the desert to spread at the edges by grazing too many animals there and reducing the vegetation cover. Africa's rich and varied birdlife is also threatened by people cutting down forests, draining marshes and swamps, and building farms and cities.

CLIMATE AND LANDSCAPE

Most of Africa has a hot climate, with large areas that receive very little rain, especially the Sahara Desert in the north and the Namib and Kalahari in the southwest. The wettest areas are near the Equator in the center of the continent. Unlike other continents, Africa has few mountain chains. Generally, there are high flat plains sometimes broken by a single mountain, such as Kilimanjaro, in Tanzania, East Africa.

AFRICA ON THE MOVE

Africa has not always been in the position it is in today. Like all the other continents, it has gradually shifted around the Earth as a result of movements in the Earth's surface or crust. Africa was once joined to the other continents but, over millions of years, it has drifted away. African birds evolved into many unique species because they could not mix with birds from other continents.

About 130 million years ago Africa began to split away from the other continents and became a single continent. At that time, Madagascar was still joined to mainland Africa. Later, it drifted away to become an island, so the birdlife there developed separately from that in Africa.

In the last 100 million years Africa has drifted toward Europe to its position on today's globe.

AMAZING BIRDS OF AFRICA

Red-billed Quelea
(*Quelea quelea*)

Most abundant bird
There are more red-billed queleas in the world than any other bird. Feeding flocks may contain millions of birds and colonies and can have up to 10 million nests.

Longest toes
The African jacana has the longest toes of any bird. They are up to 3 in (8 cm) long.

Highest flier
A Rüppell's Griffon Vulture collided with a plane when flying over the coast of West Africa at an altitude of 36,988 ft (11,274 m). This is the highest altitude at which a bird has ever been identified.

Broadest bill
The Shoebill, or Whale-headed Stork, has the broadest bill of any bird – 5 in (12 cm) wide.

Largest bird
The African Ostrich is the world's largest and tallest bird. Males can be up to 9 ft (2.7 m) tall and weigh as much as 344 lb (156 kg). The ostrich also lays the largest eggs. The eggs are so tough that a person can stand on one of them without breaking it.

African Ostrich
(*Struthio camelus*)

EUROPE

MEDITERRANEAN SEA

Nile

RED SEA

ARABIAN PENINSULA

ATLAS MTS

HOGGAR MTS

SAHARA DESERT

TIBESTI

A F R I C A

Niger

Lake Chad

FACTS ABOUT AFRICA

Number of birds

About 1,700 species of bird live in Africa. Kenya has a particularly rich birdlife, with more than 1,000 different species.

Deep lake

Lake Tanganyika is 4,708 ft (1,435 m) deep and is the second deepest lake in the world. Africa's largest lake is Lake Victoria, but it is only 266 ft (81 m) deep.

Longest river

The Nile is 4,170 miles (6,670 km) long. It is the world's longest river.

Spectacular waterfall

The Victoria Falls on the River Zambezi drop 355 ft (108 m) over a ledge 5,580 ft (1,700 m) wide.

Biggest desert

The Sahara is the biggest desert in the world – about 3,474,927 sq miles (9 million sq km). The world's highest sand dunes occur in the Sahara. They can be up to 1,410 ft (430 m) high.

Colossal crack

The Great Rift Valley is about 4,000 miles (6,400 km) long, and in some parts it is 22-37 miles (35-60 km) wide. It was formed about 25 million years ago, when land slipped down between huge cracks, probably with the movements of the Earth's crust.

These storm clouds signal the start of the rainy season on the Tanzanian grasslands. Some African birds migrate from place to place within Africa, following the rains.

TYPICAL BIRDS

Here are just a few examples of typical birds from the most important habitats of Africa. These range from hot dry deserts and open grasslands to warm humid rain forests and rivers, lakes, and swamps. You can find out more about typical African birds and where they live on the next few pages.

Islands

The Cuckoo Roller is one of many unique bird families that live only on the island of Madagascar. Others include the ground rollers, asities, and vanga shrikes.

Savannah

There are only two species of oxpecker in the world. Both live on the African savannah. Oxpeckers live on insects, which they take from the skin of grazing animals, such as this giraffe.

Desert

Birds find it hard to survive in a dry desert habitat, but Sandgrouse can fly long distances to waterholes to find water. They exist on a diet of dry seeds.

Rainforests

This Pitta is a common bird of the rain forests. African rain forests used to be more widespread. Now they have shrunk, as the climate became drier and people have cut the trees down.

Mountains

Birds of prey, such as this Verreaux's Eagle, thrive in the African mountains, where they can soar aloft rising air currents and spot their prey running on the bare ground below.

Lakes and rivers

Kingfishers, such as this Pied Kingfisher, are a common sight around African lakes and rivers, which are rich in food and nesting places.

Marshes and swamps

Large numbers of fish-eating birds, such as this Goliath Heron, live and feed in vast tropical swamplands such as the Okavango Delta in southern Africa.

ETHIOPIAN PLATEAU

INDIAN OCEAN

MADAGASCAR

Lake Victoria

Lake Tanganyika

GREAT RIFT VALLEY

Lake Nyasa

Congo

Zambezi

KALAHARI DESERT

NAMIB DESERT

ATLANTIC OCEAN

Forests and Mountains

STRETCHING ACROSS the center of Africa is the second largest area of rain forest in the world. It grows in the tropical regions around the Equator, where the climate is hot and wet all year round. A variety of birds, such as hornbills, turacos, and pittas, thrive in this rich environment, where there are plenty of leaves, fruits, and insects to eat and trees and bushes to nest in. Areas of rain forest also grow on the lower slopes of the mountains in East Africa. On the higher slopes is a cold, misty world of grasses and giant plants, which is home to birds such as eagles and sunbirds.

The island of Madagascar off the east coast of Africa has areas of both mountain and rain forest, as well as deserts and grasslands. In this varied environment, which has been cut off from the rest of Africa for millions of years, many unique animals have evolved. These include families of birds that are not found anywhere else in the world.

GREEN WOOD HOOPOE

These birds move around in a noisy family group, probing tree trunks and branches for insect grubs with their long, curved bills. Several times every hour, the birds perform a cackling display, so that any birds that have strayed can hear where the main group is and return to it. Up to 10 green wood hoopoes help each set of parents gather food and defend the eggs and chicks. When the chicks grow up, they may become "helpers" for the adults who cared for them.

Sunbirds often feed on giant lobelia.

Scarlet-tufted Malachite Sunbird
(*Nectarinia johnstoni*)
Length: 6 in (15 cm)
Male's tail: up to 8 in (20 cm)

Both males and females puff out these red tufts to attract a mate.

The male's chest feathers turn green during the breeding season; at other times, they are brown. Tail feathers are long all year.

SCARLET-TUFTED MALACHITE SUNBIRD

This large mountain sunbird often perches on flowers, probing for sweet nectar with its long, thin, curved bill. It has strong feet and sharp claws with which to grip slippery leaves. It also eats a lot of insects, holding them in the jagged edges near the tip of its bill. As it feeds, it helps spread pollen from flower to flower. It has little flaps over its nostrils to stop pollen dust from getting up its nose.

Helmet Vanga
(*Euryceros prevostii*)
Length: 12 in (31 cm)

The strong hooked bill is used mainly for catching insects, but the helmet vanga will also eat frogs and small reptiles, such as this chameleon.

During the cackling display, the birds face each other, rocking to and fro and bowing low.

HELMET VANGA

This bird belongs to a family of birds called the vangas, found only on the island of Madagascar. There are 14 species of vanga on the island. These probably evolved over millions of years from a single species of helmet shrike, which crossed over from Africa. Each of the species lives in a different habitat, so that there are enough nest sites and food to go around.

The tail is raised high in the air when the bird displays.

Green Wood Hoopoe
(*Phoeniculus purpureus*)
Length: 15 in (38 cm)

The Yellow-billed Hornbill hops from tree to tree, feeding on insects and fruit. Hornbills and turacos feed beneath the dense rain forest canopy, out of sight of birds of prey flying above.

Legend:
- Great Blue Turaco
- Helmet Vanga
- African Pitta
- Congo Peafowl
- Trumpeter Hornbill
- Green Wood Hoopoe
- Scarlet-tufted Malachite Sunbird

AFRICA

Niger
Senegal
Blue Nile
White Nile
RED SEA
Congo
Lake Victoria
ATLANTIC OCEAN
Congo
Kasai
GREAT RIFT VALLEY
Lake Tanganyika
Lake Nyasa
Zambezi
Lake Kariba
KALAHARI DESERT
Limpopo
MOZAMBIQUE CHANNEL
MADAGASCAR
Orange River
DRAKENSBERG MTS
INDIAN OCEAN

| 0 | 250 | 500 | 750 km |
| 0 | 250 | 500 miles |

Giant groundsels grow high on the African mountains. Sunbirds nest among their cabbage-like leaves.

The casque on top of the bill is light and spongy inside. Males, like this bird, have larger casques than those of females.

With its large curved bill, the bird can reach fruit in the trees and toss it into its mouth.

Trumpeter Hornbill
(Ceratogymna bucinator)
Length: 2 ft 2 in (66 cm)

Great Blue Turaco
(Corythaeola cristata)
Length: 2 ft 6 in (76 cm)

GREAT BLUE TURACO
Groups of up to 12 great blue turacos run and climb through the treetops. They feed on fruits, including berries that are poisonous to people. The nest is a flimsy platform of twigs built in a tall tree. When very young, chicks scramble about on the nest using tiny claws on their wings to keep their balance. After about four weeks, they leave the nest for good, but it is several days before they can fly.

TRUMPETER HORNBILL
The loud, wailing call of the Trumpeter Hornbill sounds like a child crying. Hornbills have very unusual nesting habits. The male builds a round nest inside a hole in a tree, then seals the opening, leaving the female inside. The male passes food to her through a narrow slit. This temporary "prison" protects the female and her chicks from enemies.

African Pitta
(Pitta angolensis)
Length: 7 in (18 cm)

AFRICAN PITTA
The shy, tiny African Pitta hops through dense undergrowth on the rain forest floor, searching for slugs and insects. Although it is brightly colored, the bird blends in surprisingly well with the leafy forest background. To threaten enemies, it crouches down with its wings spread and its bill pointing upward.

Only males have this tuft of white bristles.

CONGO PEAFOWL
This unusual bird is the only true African pheasant – all the others originally came from Asia. Unlike other pheasants, such as the common peafowl (peacock), the Congo Peafowl has a short tail. It lives on the rain forest floor, feeding on fruits and insects. Both parents probably help take care of the eggs and young.

Both males and females have bright, shiny feathers.

Congo Peafowl
(Afropavo congensis)
Length: 2 ft 4 in (71 cm)

The Savannah

THE DRY, GRASSY PLAINS of the savannah provide food for a variety of seed- and insect-eating birds. Some of these birds are closely linked to the mammals of the grasslands. Oxpeckers, for instance, cling to giraffes, zebras, rhinos, and other animals with their sharp claws, while snapping up ticks and other blood-sucking parasites. Vultures and marabou storks help clean up the carcasses left by lions and other big cats.

In some parts of the savannah, trees such as the flat-topped acacias can be used as nest sites by birds such as weavers, starlings, or rollers. Other small birds hide their nests on the ground. The savannah has a wet season and a dry season. Birds tend to raise their young after the rains, when the grasses are green and lush and there is plenty of food. Unfortunately, savannah birdlife is increasingly threatened by people who live on and farm the remaining grasslands.

SECRETARY BIRD

This bird was so-named because its crest makes it look like an old-fashioned secretary with a quill pen stuck behind its ear. It feeds on small mammals, insects, and some birds and their eggs. It can also kill snakes. The Secretary Bird snaps up small animals in its sharp bill but kills larger ones by stamping on them. During courtship, the birds fly up high making strange calls. The nest is a platform of sticks, built at the top of a tree.

Secretary Bird
(*Sagittarius serpentarius*)
Length: 5 ft (1.5 m)

The head crest is often raised while the bird is hunting.

Long legs enable it to walk easily through the tall grasses.

Hooked bill tears flesh from food.

Martial Eagle
(*Polemaetus bellicosus*)
Length: 2 ft 8 in (83 cm)

Very strong, curved talons kill prey.

0   400   800   1,200 km

0   400   800 miles

ATLAS MT

SAHARA

Niger

MARTIAL EAGLE

This is the largest and most powerful eagle in Africa. A female may have a wingspan of 8 ft 5 in (2.6 m). The eagle swoops down from great heights at high speed to attack its prey, or it may lie in wait to ambush prey from a branch. The Martial Eagle builds its nest in tall trees. Females usually lay just one egg.

Masai Ostrich
(*Struthio camelus*)
Length: 8 ft 2 in (2.5 m)
Height: 8 ft 2 in (2.5 m)

Ostriches are the only birds with two toes on each foot.

Strong legs and toes enable it to run at up to 43 mph (70 kph)

MASAI OSTRICH

This enormous ostrich is the largest bird alive today. It strides effortlessly across the grassy plains, using its sharp eyes to search for leaves, seeds, and insects. The male makes a nest by scraping a hollow in the ground. Several females lay their eggs in one nest.

VULTURES

High above the African grasslands, white-backed vultures like these soar on outstretched wings. The vulture uses its keen eyesight to find a carcass and glides down slowly to feed. It also watches out for other vultures swooping down, as this means there is a dead animal nearby.

VILLAGE WEAVER

Village weavers live in flocks and build their nests together, so that they are safer from attack. There may be as many as 100 nests in a single tree. The male builds the nest from strips of grass, which he weaves into a round ball. He starts by building a swing to perch on, then makes a ring shape, and finally a round ball. To attract a female, a male hangs upside down from the nest, flicking his wings. If a female likes the nest, she lays her eggs there and raises her young by herself.

These Village Weaver nests are at the tips of branches where enemies such as snakes cannot reach them.

Paradise Whydah
(*Vidua paradisaea*)
Length: male: 16 in (41 cm);
female: 5 in (13 cm)

The male holds his two short, wide tail feathers up above long tail feathers during his display flights.

The weaver loops and knots grass together to make the nest, rather like basket weaving.

Village Weaver
(*Ploceus cucullatus*)
Length: 7 in (18 cm)

Male village weavers may steal green grass from each other's nests.

DESERT

AFRICA

Nile

Lake Chad

Congo

ATLANTIC OCEAN

Zambezi

PARADISE WHYDAH

To impress a female or ward off rivals, the male Paradise Whydah shows off his remarkable tail. The whydah does not take care of its young. Instead, the female lays her eggs in the nest of a Melba Finch – a kind of waxbill to which the whydahs are related. Young whydahs have the same colors inside their mouths as young finches. This is why the foster parents feed the whydah chicks as if they were their own.

The female is a dull brown.

The male grows tail feathers up to 11 in (28 cm) long during the breeding season.

Honeyguides have a very thick skin to protect them against bee stings.

Carmine bee-eaters live in colonies of hundreds of birds. They dig burrows in the soil, often in vertical banks.

GREATER HONEYGUIDE

The honeyguide leads people or honey badgers to bees' nests. Once the "helper" opens up the nest, the birds can feast on the honey. The female lays her eggs in the nests of other birds – one egg in each nest. The young honeyguides attack and kill the other young with a hook on their bills.

Honeyguides have special calling places, where they often perch.

The central tail feathers are up to 5 in (13 cm) long.

Southern Carmine Bee-eater
(*Merops nubicus nubicoides*)
Length: 15 in (38 cm)

SOUTHERN CARMINE BEE-EATER

The carmine bee-eater may perch on the back of an ostrich, stork, goat, or sheep, snatching up insects disturbed by its feet. It also gathers near grass fires, where it eats up the insects trying to escape from the flames. The bee-eater specializes in eating stinging insects. To get rid of the sting, it holds the insect tightly in its bill and beats and rubs it against a perch. Then it swallows the insect whole.

Greater Honeyguide
(*Indicator indicator*)
Length: 8 in (20 cm).

Wetlands

AFRICA'S TROPICAL WETLANDS include great rivers such as the Nile, the Volta, and the Niger, as well as vast swamps such as the Sudd and the Okavango Delta. These swamps, and the marshes that surround the great rivers, teem with life, especially fish. Large numbers of fish-eating birds live there, including herons, egrets, ibises, storks, and pelicans. Reeds and rafts of lilies growing in the warm, shallow waters also provide nest sites and safe places to feed.

In the east of Africa lies the Great Rift Valley. This long, narrow valley has formed where a section of the Earth's crust is slowly splitting, causing the land in between to sink. The walls of the rift valley tower high above the flat valley floor which contains many spectacular lakes. Birds from Europe and Asia use the African wetlands as resting places on their journeys across the continent, looking for somewhere to spend the winter.

Fish Eagle
(Haliaeetus vocifer)
Length: 2 ft 6 in (76 cm)

Courting males and females show off their flying skills – they try to grab each other's talons as they tumble downward through the air.

FISH EAGLE

This bird's loud, gull-like scream rings through the African wetlands. It perches in tall trees near water and swoops down to snatch fish in its powerful claws. Sometimes it plunges underwater feet first and then rises up, lifting the fish clear out of the water.

BLACK HERON		FISH EAGLE
HAMMERKOP		PEL'S FISHING OWL
AFRICAN JACANA		WHALE-HEADED STORK
LESSER FLAMINGO		

Pel's Fishing Owl
(Scotopelia peli)
Length: 2 ft (61 cm)

Large eyes help the owl see well in the dark.

PEL'S FISHING OWL

During the day, Pel's Fishing Owl hides away in trees near rivers and swamps. At night, it swoops low over the water and catches fish in its powerful feet. Its legs and feet are bare; this way, no feathers trailing in the water could get wet and soggy. Unlike other owls, Pel's Fishing Owl does not have fringed feathers and soft plumage for silent flight; it does not need to fly quietly to sneak up on fish.

The feet have small spikes underneath, to grip slippery fish or frogs.

AFRICA

Lake Tana
GULF OF ADEN
Niger
SUDD
White Nile
Lake Volta
Lake Turkana
Congo
GREAT RIFT VALLEY
Lake Victoria
ATLANTIC OCEAN
Congo
Lake Tanganyika
Lake Nyasa
INDIAN OCEAN
Zambezi
OKAVANGO DELTA
KALAHARI DESERT
Limpopo
Orange River

Millions of flamingos flock to Rift Valley lakes, such as Lake Turkana, to feed on microscopic plants and animals growing there.

0	300	600	900 km
0		300	600 miles

The Okavango Delta is a vast wetland area, where storks and pelicans live alongside hippopotamuses and buffaloes.

HAMMERKOP

Hammerkop
(Scopus umbretta)
Length: 1 ft 10 in (56 cm)

This strange-looking bird is named after its hammer-shaped head. It builds a huge, roofed nest of twigs, grass, and mud, usually high in a tree near water. The nest is decorated with feathers, bones, and snakeskins, with garbage that people have thrown away. It is strong enough for a person to stand on the roof without falling in. Chicks are safe inside its thick walls while the parents find food.

Each nest takes 1-6 months to build, but hammerkops often build several nests each year. No one knows why they do this.

With its short tail and large wings, it glides and soars easily.

BLACK HERON

The Black Heron, or egret, fishes for food in an unusual way. It spreads its wings out around its head to shade the water. The reason for this could be that the shaded area makes it easier for the bird to see fish by cutting out reflections on the surface of the water. Another explanation is that fish may swim into the dark patch, thinking it is a safe shelter. When the heron spots a fish, it jabs its bill quickly into the water to grab a meal.

Black Heron
(Egretta ardesiaca)
Length: up to 3 ft 2 in (1 m)

The toes are partly webbed.

It makes an "umbrella" over the water with its wings for 2-3 seconds at a time, by day or night.

It uses its long, thin bill to stab prey.

The huge head supports the massive bill.

Large eyes help the bird spot fish and other prey in the water.

The hook at the tip of the bill grabs hold of wet, slippery food.

Whale-headed Stork
(Balaeniceps rex)
Length: 3 ft 9 in (1.2 m)

WHALE-HEADED STORK

Another common name for this bird is the shoebill, because of its extraordinary shoe-shaped bill. The huge bill helps the bird catch and hold its favorite food – lungfish. It also eats young crocodiles, turtles, frogs, and snakes. Parents sometimes collect water in their bills and pour it over their chicks in hot weather, to keep them cool.

LESSER FLAMINGO

Thousands of these flamingos flock to African lakes to nest and to feed on tiny water plants. To make sure the chicks get enough food, the parents produce a kind of rich "milk" in their *crop* – a pouch in the wall of the gut. The milk is bright red because it is dyed with pink pigment in the food they eat, which includes pink mollusks. Their feathers are pink for the same reason.

Lesser Flamingo
(Phoeniconaius minor)
Length: 3 ft 4 in (1 m)

African Jacana
(Actophilornis africanus)
Length: 11 in (28 cm)

Chicks make begging calls when they are hungry.

Long toes and claws spread out the bird's weight, so it can walk on floating plants without sinking.

AFRICAN JACANA

These birds are also called lilytrotters. They run over floating plants, pecking at the water and leaves to collect food. The male builds the nest, sits on the eggs, and takes care of the chicks. This is very rare behavior for a male bird because female birds usually raise the young.

Asia

ASIA IS THE LARGEST CONTINENT in the world. Much of northern, central, and southwest Asia has a cold, dry climate, with harsh deserts, dry grasslands, and frozen forests which few birds can survive. Many birds are forced to migrate south during colder seasons. The warm, rainy, tropical lands of Southeast Asia are, however, home to a spectacular variety of birds, including pheasants, babblers, flycatchers, warblers, and thrushes. Some birds, such as the Golden-fronted Leafbird, the Great Argus Pheasant, and the Rhinoceros Hornbill, are found nowhere else in the world.

To the west, Asia is joined to Europe and Africa. Some of the birds of Asia are the same as, or similar to, birds in these continents. To the south, the islands of Southeast Asia form of stepping stones along which birds can move to and from New Guinea and Australia.

About half the people in the world live in Asia. They have made major changes to the land and plant life across the continent. Birds are increasingly threatened by the spread of cities and by forest destruction. Unless birds can adapt to an urban lifestyle, they have nowhere to live when their natural homes are destroyed.

INDIA ON THE MOVE
Over millions of years, continental drift has caused India to move into different positions on the globe.

About 200 million years ago
India was joined to Africa, Australia, and Antarctica. But it split away on its own and slowly began to drift northward to Asia (right).

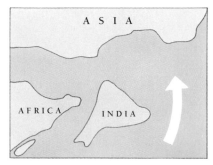

About 60-40 million years ago
India crashed into Asia, pushing up land from under the sea to create the gigantic folds of land that form the Himalayan Mountains. India is still pushing into Asia at a rate of about 0.6 miles (1 km) every 100,000 years.

CLIMATE AND LANDSCAPE
The great Asian mountain chains, such as the Karakoram, Pamirs, and Himalayas, cut across Asia from east to west, separating the warmer, wetter lands of India and Southeast Asia from the cooler, drier lands of Central Asia. Southeast Asia is made mainly of thousands of islands, many of which were formed by volcanoes erupting through the seabed.

Many Southeast Asian islands, such as these in Indonesia, have a monsoon climate, with heavy rain in summer and cooler, drier winters. Seasons are altered by strong winds.

AMAZING BIRDS OF ASIA

Loudest woodpecker
This enormous woodpecker can be heard hammering at tree trunks from up to 1.12 miles (1.8 km) away.

Black Woodpecker
(*Dryocopis martius*)

Most chatty bird
The Hill Mynah is the world's most talkative caged bird.

Heaviest head
The Helmeted Hornbill has a solid ivory casque on top of its bill, which gives it the heaviest bill of any bird.

Biggest tail
The Crested Argus Pheasant has the longest and largest tail in the world. A male's tail feathers can reach 5 ft 8 in (1.73 m) long and 5 in (13 cm) wide.

Quickest chicks
The chicks of the Cabot's Tragopan are the quickest to fly after hatching. They grow all their flight feathers within 24 hours of hatching and can flutter up into the trees immediately.

Heaviest flier
The Great Bustard is the world's heaviest flying bird. Males can weigh up to 40 lb (18 kg) – as much as a small child.

Great Bustard
(*Otis tarda*)

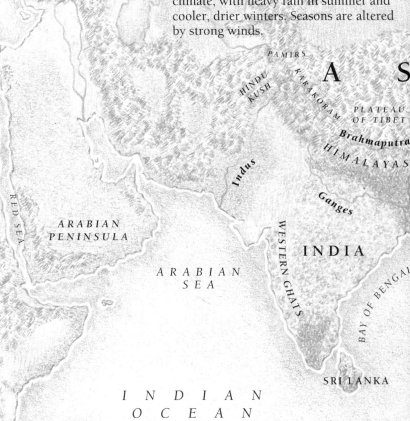

FACTS ABOUT ASIA

Highest mountains
The Himalayas are the world's highest mountain range and contain the highest point on Earth – Mount Everest – which reaches 29,028 ft (8,848 m).

Number of birds
About 1,900 species of bird live in tropical mainland Asia, Sri Lanka, Sumatra, Java, Borneo, Taiwan, Hainan, and the Philippines. More than 300 species breed in the Philippines alone.

Biggest forest
The conifer forests of northern Asia, called the taiga, cover more than 4.5 million sq miles (12 million sq km) from Scandinavia in the west to the coast of the Pacific Ocean in the east. The taiga is the largest forest in the world.

Most volcanoes
Java in Indonesia has about 50 volcanoes. Mount Bromo (below) is the biggest of them. Volcanic soils cover about 16 percent of Japan.

Largest delta
The delta of the Ganges and Brahmaputra rivers in India covers an area of 23,000 sq miles (60,000 sq km).

Deepest lake on Earth
Lake Baikal in Siberia is the largest lake in Asia. It is 5,317 ft (1,637 m) deep and contains one-fifth of all the fresh water on Earth.

Highest rainfall
Cherrapunji in India has the highest rainfall in the world – 425 in (10,800 mm) in a year.

TYPICAL BIRDS

Here are just a few examples of typical birds from the most important habitats of Asia. You can find out more about typical birds and their habitats on the next few pages.

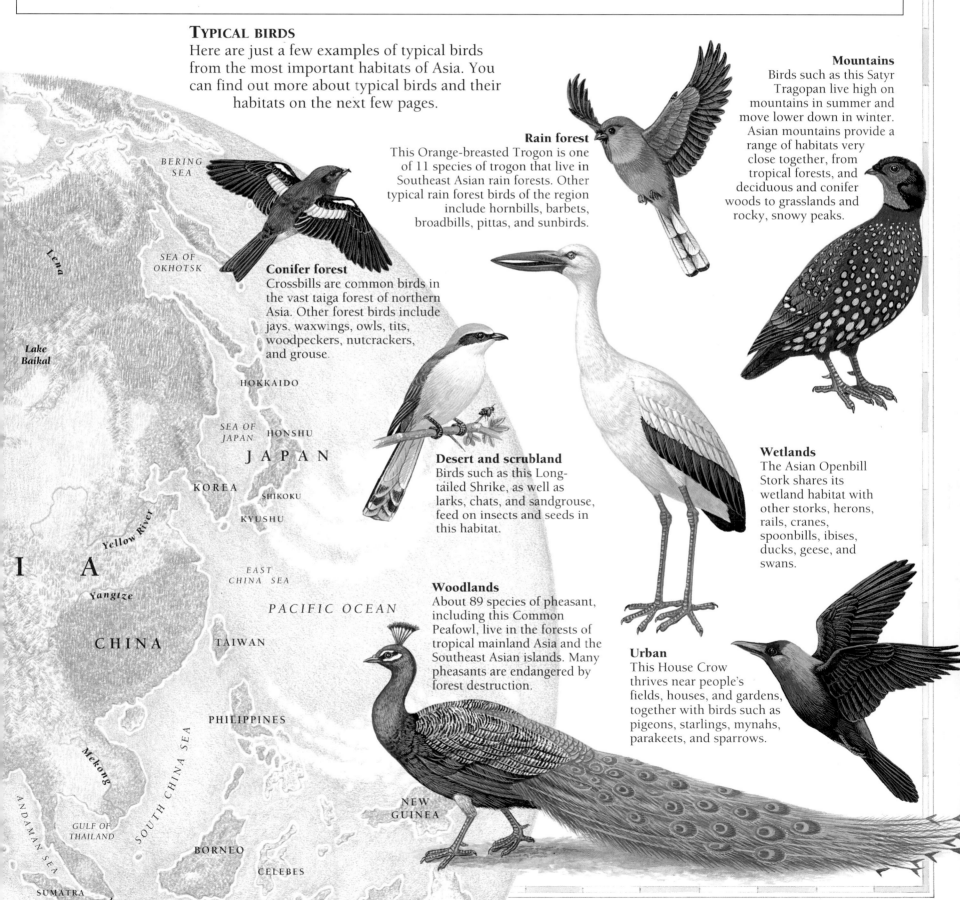

Rain forest
This Orange-breasted Trogon is one of 11 species of trogon that live in Southeast Asian rain forests. Other typical rain forest birds of the region include hornbills, barbets, broadbills, pittas, and sunbirds.

Mountains
Birds such as this Satyr Tragopan live high on mountains in summer and move lower down in winter. Asian mountains provide a range of habitats very close together, from tropical forests, and deciduous and conifer woods to grasslands and rocky, snowy peaks.

Conifer forest
Crossbills are common birds in the vast taiga forest of northern Asia. Other forest birds include jays, waxwings, owls, tits, woodpeckers, nutcrackers, and grouse.

Desert and scrubland
Birds such as this Long-tailed Shrike, as well as larks, chats, and sandgrouse, feed on insects and seeds in this habitat.

Wetlands
The Asian Openbill Stork shares its wetland habitat with other storks, herons, rails, cranes, spoonbills, ibises, ducks, geese, and swans.

Woodlands
About 89 species of pheasant, including this Common Peafowl, live in the forests of tropical mainland Asia and the Southeast Asian islands. Many pheasants are endangered by forest destruction.

Urban
This House Crow thrives near people's fields, houses, and gardens, together with birds such as pigeons, starlings, mynahs, parakeets, and sparrows.

BERING SEA

Lena

SEA OF OKHOTSK

Lake Baikal

HOKKAIDO

SEA OF JAPAN

HONSHU

JAPAN

KOREA

SHIKOKU

KYUSHU

Yellow River

EAST CHINA SEA

PACIFIC OCEAN

I A

Yangtze

CHINA

TAIWAN

PHILIPPINES

Mekong

ANDAMAN SEA

GULF OF THAILAND

SOUTH CHINA SEA

BORNEO

CELEBES

NEW GUINEA

SUMATRA

INDONESIA

JAVA

AUSTRALIA

The Himalayas

FROM THE FROZEN snow-covered peaks down to the hot forests on the lower slopes, the huge Himalayan Mountains provide a wide range of habitats for birds. At the top of the mountains, the bitterly cold weather and steep rocky slopes cause the death of many animals, so lammergeiers, vultures, ravens, and other birds that eat dead animals, have a steady food supply. During the warmer summer months, flower meadows farther down the slopes are alive with buzzing insects. Accentors and redstarts eagerly snap these up, while the pigeons and partridges that also feed in these high meadows prefer to eat shoots and bulbs.
Many birds spend the summer feeding and nesting high up the mountains but fly down to the sheltered forests in the foothills for the winter. These forests are rich in fruits and seeds and teem with mynahs, babblers, and parakeets. Unfortunately, many Himalayan forests have been cut down for firewood or to make way for farms. With fewer trees to soak up the rain and keep the soil firmly in place, water pours down the mountains into the valleys, causing serious floods.

Bar-headed Goose
(*Anser indicus*)
Length: 2 ft 5 in (75 cm)

Flocks of geese fly in the shape of the letter "V," so that the wind flows past them more easily and doesn't hold them back.

Lammergeier
(*Gypaetus barbatus*)
Length: 3 ft 3 in (1 m)
Wingspan: up to 9 ft (2.7 m)

BAR-HEADED GOOSE
This goose breeds in Central Asia and migrates over the Himalayas to spend the winter in India. It rests by day near rivers and lakes. At night it grazes in fields of crops, so farmers often shoot at it. As it flies from one feeding ground to another, the Bar-headed Goose makes a wild musical honking sound.

LAMMERGEIER
The acrobatic Lammergeier, or Bearded Vulture, glides and soars over the high mountain slopes, searching for skeletons that have been picked clean by its cousin, the Griffon Vulture. The Lammergeier feeds on the marrow inside bones. The bird flies up to great heights and drops the bones onto rocks to smash them apart. It may drop one bone up to 50 times before breaking it. A Lammergeier will return to the same site year after year to crack open bones, and occasionally tortoise shells, in this way.

The long thin tongue is shaped like a garden trowel for scooping marrow from bones.

Stiff black feathers hang down like a "beard."

HIMALAYAN MONAL PHEASANT
WHITE-CHEEKED BULBUL
INDIAN HILL MYNAH
BAR-HEADED GOOSE
LAMMERGEIER
WALLCREEPER
HIMALAYAN SNOWCOCK

Brahmaputra

Ganges

INDIA

HIMALAYAS

Indus

HINDU KUSH

Indus

WALLCREEPER
The nimble Wallcreeper climbs up sheer walls of rock, probing for insects with its curved pointed bill. It often spreads out its wings to keep itself propped up while it searches. In summer, the Wallcreeper moves high up the mountains, but in winter, it moves down to the shelter of the lower slopes. Birders have fun lying on their backs, watching the high cliffs for returning wallcreepers.

Because it flutters its wings like a butterfly, it is also known as the "Butterfly Bird."

The male has a black throat in summer.

Wallcreeper
(*Tichodroma muraria*)
Length: 6 in (15 cm)

450 km

300 miles

300

150

150

0

0

Irrawaddy

BAY OF BENGAL

Male

Female's brown feathers help camouflage her on the nest.

Female

Short strong legs are ideal for mountain climbing.

HIMALAYAN MONAL PHEASANT

This pheasant lives in the forests and meadows of the Himalayas, moving up and down the mountains with the seasons. It uses its powerful curved bill as a digging tool to uncover roots, bulbs, and insect grubs. To display to a female, the male raises his crest, fluffs out his shiny neck feathers, fans his tail, and droops his wings. In many areas, these pheasants are threatened with extinction caused by hunting.

Himalayan Monal Pheasant
(*Lophophorus impejanus*)
Length: 2 ft 3 in (70 cm)

A male Common Peafowl displays his magnificent feathers. Many other spectacular pheasants live in the forests of the Himalayas.

Indian Hill Mynah
(*Gracula religiosa*)
Length: 11 in (28 cm)

INDIAN HILL MYNAH

The noisy Hill Mynah lives in the tops of forest trees on the lower mountain slopes, feeding mainly on fruits and nectar. It makes a wide variety of whistling calls and is a brilliant mimic of the human voice. People have taken many of these birds from the wild to be kept as "talking" pets.

Bright yellow face wattles (folds of skin) stand out against the glossy black feathers.

INDIAN OCEAN

EASTERN GHATS

Godavari

DECCAN PLATEAU

Narmada

S R I L A N K A

WESTERN GHATS

GULF OF KHAMBHAT

Himalayan Snowcock
(*Tetraogallus himalayensis*)
Length: 1 ft 10 in (56 cm)

White-cheeked Bulbul
(*Pycnonotus leucogenys*)
Length: 8 in (20 cm)

The Himalayan race of this bulbul has a long crest.

WHITE-CHEEKED BULBUL

This lively bulbul lives as high up as 7,000 ft (2,100 m) in the Himalayas. It often perches on the tops of bushes, bowing, flicking its tail, and calling loudly. The White-cheeked Bulbul is not afraid of people. It is an inquisitive bird that lives near villages and towns and sometimes goes right inside houses to steal food. (You can find his cousin, the Red-whiskered Bulbul, in South Florida.)

Flocks of birds, such as these snow pigeons, fly at very high altitudes across the snow-covered peaks of the Himalayas.

HIMALAYAN SNOWCOCK

The mottled colors of the Himalayan Snowcock blend in well with the rocks and snow on the high mountain slopes. This bird eats all sorts of plant material, including roots, tubers, berries, shoots, and seeds, but it often has to search large areas to find enough to eat. During the breeding season, males make whistling calls to impress females.

Short wings and a long tail are characteristic of bulbuls.

Southeast Asia

BETWEEN THE SOUTHERN EDGE of mainland Asia and northern Australasia is an area of shallow seas dotted with thousands of islands. On the islands nearest Australia and New Guinea, Asian and Australasian birds mix together. On more remote islands, such as the Philippines, many unique birds have developed away from contact with other species.

There are many volcanoes in southeast Asia, and some of the islands are in fact the tops of giant underwater volcanoes. The rich volcanic soils and hot humid climate in this region have encouraged the growth of lush rain forests. A huge variety of birds live in these rain forests, where there are lots of insects, fruits, and seeds to eat. Great numbers of birds often gather in the fruit-bearing trees, but they are well camouflaged and hard to see in the depths of the forest. Many people live in this region, and much of the original rain forest has been cleared to make way for villages, towns, mines, and farms. This leaves the birds with nowhere to live and threatens the survival of many species.

Deep hooked bill is used to rip open prey.

Monkey-eating Eagle
(Pithecophaga jefferyi)
Length: 3 ft 1 in (95 cm)

MONKEY-EATING EAGLE

This fierce eagle glides over the treetops or swoops down from a perch to catch its prey. It hunts monkeys and flying lemurs (called colugos), as well as small deer and large birds such as hornbills. The Monkey-eating Eagle is one of the rarest birds of prey (raptors) in the world because of the destruction of its forest home. Only a few hundred of these birds survive in the wild.

Flying lemurs (colugos) are a favorite food.

There are two very long feathers in the middle of the tail.

The male fans out his stunning wing feathers to impress a female.

HORNBILLS

Hornbills are named for the strange hornlike growth, called a casque, which many of them have atop their bills. It is made of a thin layer of skin and bone over a light "honeycomb" structure. No one really knows what the casque is for. It may help one hornbill tell the sex and age of another, or it may make the bird's call louder.

Great Indian Hornbill
(Buceros bicornis)
This species has a large yellow casque and a loud roaring call.

Helmeted Hornbill
(Rhinoplax vigil)
This is the only species of hornbill to have a solid casque, made of a substance like ivory.

Rhinoceros Hornbill
(Buceros rhinoceros)
Casque turns up at the end like a rhino's horn.

Rufous-necked Hornbill
(Aceros nipalensis)
This hornbill has no casque at all.

GREAT ARGUS PHEASANT

During the breeding season, the male Great Argus Pheasant clears his own patch of space on the forest floor, removing every leaf, twig, and pebble. Then he struts up and down, calling loudly to attract a female. If one arrives, he dances in front of her, spreading out his long wing feathers, which are decorated with dazzling golden eyespots.

Great Argus Pheasant
(Argusianus argus)
Length: male (including tail) 6 ft 2 in (190 cm); female 2 ft 1 in (63 cm)

Edible-nest Swiftlet
(Aerodramus fuciphagus)
Length: 4 in (10 cm)

Nests are made of saliva.

EDIBLE-NEST SWIFTLET

Thousands of these swiftlets nest in caves along the coasts or in tropical rain forests. Those that live in caves use cup-shaped nests made almost entirely out of their own saliva, which hardens like cement. The nests are stuck to the walls and roofs of the caves. People collect these nests to make "bird's nest soup," so they have become valuable.

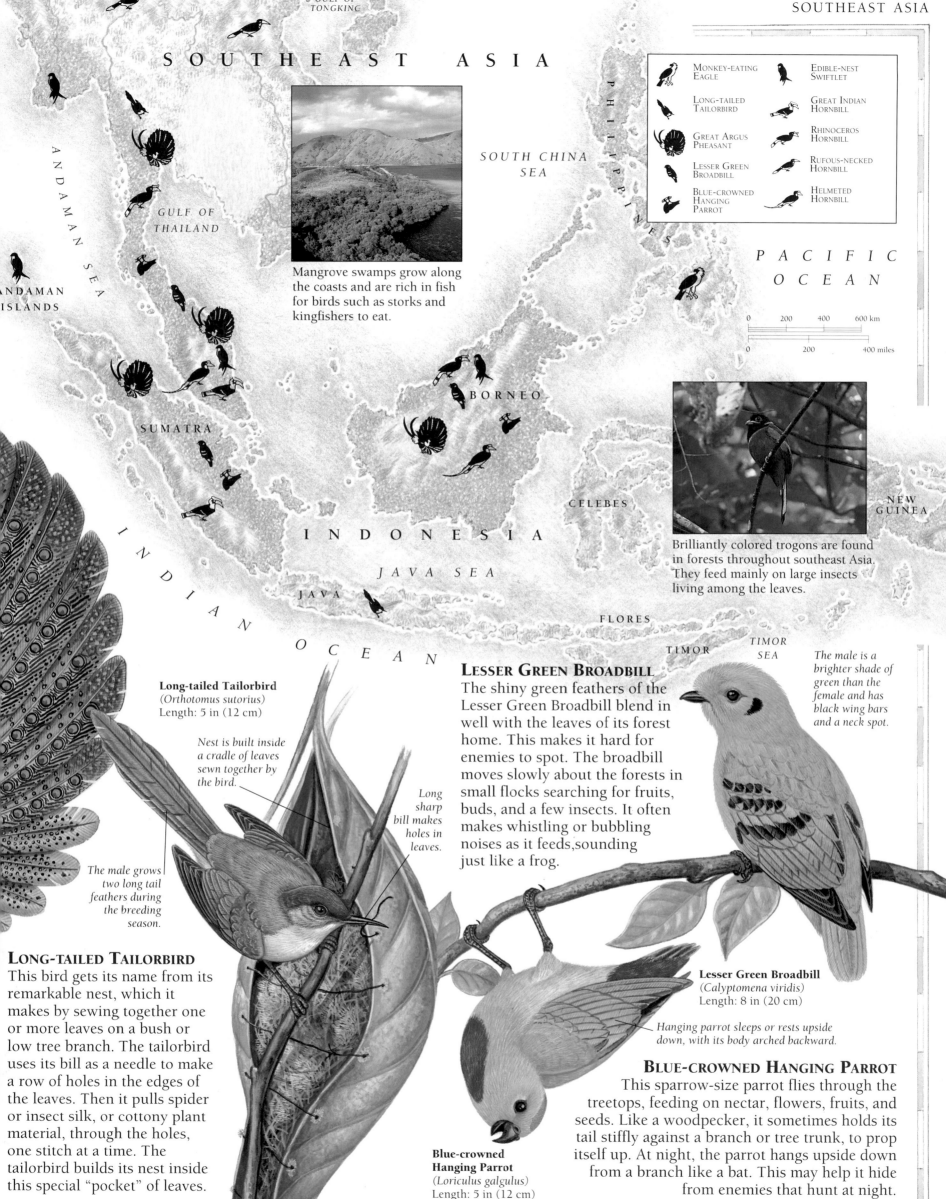

S O U T H E A S T   A S I A

GULF OF TONGKING

ANDAMAN SEA

ANDAMAN ISLANDS

GULF OF THAILAND

SUMATRA

INDIAN OCEAN

JAVA

INDONESIA

JAVA SEA

BORNEO

CELEBES

FLORES

TIMOR

TIMOR SEA

SOUTH CHINA SEA

PHILIPPINES

PACIFIC OCEAN

NEW GUINEA

Mangrove swamps grow along the coasts and are rich in fish for birds such as storks and kingfishers to eat.

Brilliantly colored trogons are found in forests throughout southeast Asia. They feed mainly on large insects living among the leaves.

Key:
- Monkey-eating Eagle
- Long-tailed Tailorbird
- Great Argus Pheasant
- Lesser Green Broadbill
- Blue-crowned Hanging Parrot
- Edible-nest Swiftlet
- Great Indian Hornbill
- Rhinoceros Hornbill
- Rufous-necked Hornbill
- Helmeted Hornbill

0   200   400   600 km
0   200   400 miles

Long-tailed Tailorbird
(*Orthotomus sutorius*)
Length: 5 in (12 cm)

Nest is built inside a cradle of leaves sewn together by the bird.

Long sharp bill makes holes in leaves.

The male grows two long tail feathers during the breeding season.

LONG-TAILED TAILORBIRD

This bird gets its name from its remarkable nest, which it makes by sewing together one or more leaves on a bush or low tree branch. The tailorbird uses its bill as a needle to make a row of holes in the edges of the leaves. Then it pulls spider or insect silk, or cottony plant material, through the holes, one stitch at a time. The tailorbird builds its nest inside this special "pocket" of leaves.

LESSER GREEN BROADBILL

The shiny green feathers of the Lesser Green Broadbill blend in well with the leaves of its forest home. This makes it hard for enemies to spot. The broadbill moves slowly about the forests in small flocks searching for fruits, buds, and a few insects. It often makes whistling or bubbling noises as it feeds, sounding just like a frog.

The male is a brighter shade of green than the female and has black wing bars and a neck spot.

Lesser Green Broadbill
(*Calyptomena viridis*)
Length: 8 in (20 cm)

Hanging parrot sleeps or rests upside down, with its body arched backward.

Blue-crowned Hanging Parrot
(*Loriculus galgulus*)
Length: 5 in (12 cm)

BLUE-CROWNED HANGING PARROT

This sparrow-size parrot flies through the treetops, feeding on nectar, flowers, fruits, and seeds. Like a woodpecker, it sometimes holds its tail stiffly against a branch or tree trunk, to prop itself up. At night, the parrot hangs upside down from a branch like a bat. This may help it hide from enemies that hunt at night.

Japan and China

MILLIONS OF PEOPLE live in crowded cities in the lowland and coastal areas of Japan and China, so there are few places left for birds to live. Some, such as the Okinawa Rail and Japanese Crested Ibis, are close to extinction. But the mountains and forests inland remain home to many birds, especially pheasants and cranes.

The islands of Japan have been separated from mainland Asia for millions of years, and many birds have evolved into distinct Japanese species. The variety of birds in Japan is due partly to the different habitats, but also to the climate, which ranges from warm Kyushu in the south to cold Hokkaido in the north. In China, the forests of the southwest are a refuge for birds such as Temminck's Tragopan and the Golden Pheasant. Northern China consists of harsh deserts and grasslands, but sandgrouse and bustards survive there.

STELLER'S SEA EAGLE

The Japanese call the spectacular Steller's Sea Eagle "the great eagle." Every winter, large numbers of these birds gather in the steep wooded valleys of northeast Hokkaido. Here they are protected from the fierce winter winds at night and go out hunting for fish during the day. They swoop down to the surface of the sea to snatch fish with their powerful curved talons. Steller's sea eagles also feed on the carcasses of sea lions and other dead animals.

Steller's Sea Eagle
(Haliaeetus pelagicus)
Length: male 2 ft 11 in (88 cm);
female 3 ft 3 in (1 m)

The male has bright red patches around his eyes.

Both male and female mikado pheasants have long tails.

Mikado Pheasant
(Syrmaticus mikado)
Length: male 2 ft 11 in (88 cm)
female 1 ft 9 in (53 cm)

PENDULINE TIT

The tiny Penduline Tit lives in reed marshes. It nests in trees, usually willows. It builds an amazing hanging nest that looks like a woolly purse. Both male and female birds weave the nest, which takes about two weeks to finish. The female lays seven or eight eggs in the nest, the young birds stay in it for two to three weeks after they hatch.

Nest is woven from pieces of grass, leaves, lichens, and moss.

Penduline Tit
(Remiz pendulinus)
Length: 4 in (11 cm)

Pointed bill pokes into bark and finds insects to eat.

Japanese White-eye
(Zosterops japonica japonica)
Length: 4 in (11 cm)

MIKADO PHEASANT

This pheasant lives only on the island of Taiwan. It feeds on berries, seeds, leaves, and insects in dense forests of oak, juniper, pine, and bamboo. In spring, the female lays about five to ten eggs; it takes nearly a month for the chicks to hatch.

HARLEQUIN DUCK

This small duck lives by fast-flowing water. It spends the winter months on rocky shores but moves inland to rushing mountain streams in summer. The Harlequin Duck is a strong swimmer. It is quite at home in swift water currents and can even shoot rapids. Its shrill whistling call can easily be heard above the loud rush of the water.

Harlequin Duck
(Histrionicus histrionicus)
Length: up to 1 ft 7 in (49 cm)

JAPANESE WHITE-EYE

This white-eye lives on the Japanese island of Honshu. It flies from tree to tree in flocks, searching for insects, seeds, buds, and fruit. In summer, the white-eye soaks up nectar from flowers with the brushlike tip of its tongue. In winter, it often visits people's gardens to feed on seeds and fruit.

The male grows colorful feathers to impress a female during the breeding season.

0 250 500 750 km

0 250 500 miles

Irtysh
Ob
ALTAI MTS

ASIA

HINDU
KUSH

KUNLUN SHAN

Indus

PLATEAU
OF TIBET

HIMALAYAS

Ganges
Brahmaputra

INDIA

Salween
Mekong

ARABIAN
SEA

BAY OF
BENGAL

CHINA

Yellow River

Yangtze

HOKKAIDO

JAPAN

SEA OF
JAPAN

KOREA

EAST
CHINA SEA

HONSHU

SHIKOKU

KYUSHU

HAINAN

SOUTH
CHINA SEA

PHILIPPINES

Beautiful white whooper swans
migrate to sheltered coastal areas of
Japan for the winter. In spring they
nest by freshwater pools.

PENDULINE TIT

STELLER'S SEA EAGLE

MIKADO PHEASANT

JAPANESE
WHITE-EYE

HARLEQUIN
DUCK

PALLAS'S
SANDGROUSE

RED-CROWNED
CRANE

PALLAS'S SANDGROUSE

This sandgrouse lives in the dry deserts
and grasslands of northern China and
Central Asia. It feeds on the seeds and
shoots of plants and flies long distances
to reach water. While the chicks are
too young to fly, the male brings
water to them. He sits in water until
his belly feathers are soaked. When
he returns, the chicks drink from
his feathers.

Pallas's Sandgrouse
(*Syrrhaptes paradoxus*)
Length: up to 16 in (40 cm)

*Long pointed feathers
help this sandgrouse
fly fast.*

*Chicks drink water from
the male's feathers.*

Red-crowned Crane
(*Grus japonensis*)
Length: 3 ft 3 in (1 m)

*A pair of cranes
dance during
courtship.*

RED-CROWNED CRANE

Red-crowned cranes perform a
spectacular courtship dance that
involves leaping, bowing, and
flapping their wings. They may
even throw feathers or stones into
the air. While dancing, each pair
forms a strong partnership. Most
cranes stay with the same mate all
their lives and rarely dance once
they have chosen a partner. Each
pair defends a large breeding
territory and calls loudly, to tell
other cranes to keep out.

Australasia

AUSTRALASIA IS MADE UP of Australia (the world's smallest continent) and the islands of New Zealand and New Guinea, together with thousands of smaller Pacific islands. Australasia has been cut off from the rest of the world for millions of years, and many of the birds in the region are not found anywhere else. These include scrub-birds, lyrebirds, and the emu in Australia, bowerbirds in Australia and New Guinea, and the kiwis of New Zealand. Some birds that are common in other parts of the world are not found in Australasia, such as pheasants, woodpeckers, and finches. A number of birds migrate to Australasia to escape bad weather at certain times of year – waders fly in from the north and seabirds from the south.

Since settlers arrived in Australasia about 200 years ago, they have cleared many of the forests. The sheep, cattle, and rabbits they brought with them have destroyed many bird habitats.

AUSTRALIA ON THE MOVE
Over millions of years, continental drift has moved Australia slowly northward. About 100 million years ago, it was joined onto Antarctica. But about 50 million years ago, it split off and started to drift. For about the next 30 million years, Australia was isolated from the rest of the world, and many of its unique birds evolved. By about 10 million years ago, it had drifted close enough to Asia for some Southeast Asian birds to move into northern Australia.

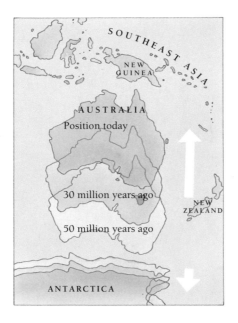

CLIMATE AND LANDSCAPE
The middle of Australia, called the outback, consists mainly of desert and has a hot, dry climate, but the southern coasts are cooler and wetter. A tropical climate, with warm, wet weather all year round, occurs in northeast Australia and in New Guinea. New Zealand is cooler, with a temperate climate. The seasons in this southern part of the world are opposite those in the north. For instance, when it is summer in Europe, it is winter in Australasia.

AMAZING BIRDS OF AUSTRALASIA

Speedy sleeper
The Spine-tailed Swift flies at speeds of up to 62 mph (100 kph) and can sleep while flying through the air.

Strong scent
The male Musk Duck has a strange pouch of skin under his bill, which he uses to impress a female during his courtship display. The bird's name comes from the musky scent it produces during the breeding season.

Australian Pelican
(*Pelecanus conspicillatus*)

Longest bill
The Australian Pelican has the longest bill in the world. It can be up to 1 ft 7 in (47 cm) long.

Biggest nest mound
The Mallee Fowl builds a "compost heap" to keep its eggs warm until they hatch. The nest mound can be 16 ft (5 m) wide and 3 ft 3 in (1 m) deep.

Biggest birds
The Emu and Cassowary are the second and third largest birds in the world, after the ostrich. Like ostriches, emus and cassowaries are too heavy to fly.

Musk Duck
(*Biziura lobata*)

Curved bill
The Wrybill of New Zealand is the only bird with a bill that curves to the right.

FACTS ABOUT AUSTRALASIA

Largest rock
Uluru (which used to be called Ayers Rock), is the world's largest free-standing rock. It lies in central Australia and is 4 miles (6 km) long and 1.5 miles (2.4 km) wide. It towers 1,143 ft (348 m) high above the desert floor.

Number of birds
More than 1,730 species of bird live in Australasia. About 60 percent of the birds that breed in Australia do not occur anywhere else in the world.

Longest river
The Murray-Darling is the largest river system in Australia – it is about 2,330 miles (3,750 km) long.

Largest coral reef
The Great Barrier Reef, off the northeast coast of Australia, is the largest living structure on Earth. It stretches down the coast over 1,250 miles (2,000 km).

Highest geyser in the region
The Pohutu geyser, in the volcanic region of New Zealand's North Island, is a violent jet of steam and water that shoots out of the ground, reaching heights of 100 ft (30 m).

Least people
Fewer people live in Australasia than in any other continent in the world, except Antarctica. In Australia and New Zealand, sheep and cattle outnumber people by more than 10 to 1.

Flattest continent
Australia is the flattest continent. Almost two-thirds of its land surface is only 1,000-2,000 ft (300-600 m) above sea level.

Largest lake
The largest lake in the continent is Lake Eyre in Australia. The lake is often dry but can cover an area of 3,436 sq miles (8.900 sq km) when flooded.

The outback of Australia consists of dry grassland and desert. This is partly due to the Great Dividing Range in the east, which prevents moist winds from the Pacific Ocean from reaching the middle of the continent.

BORNEO CELEBES

NEW GUINEA

INDONESIA

JAVA

ARAFURA SEA

TIMOR SEA

CORAL SEA

INDIAN OCEAN

GREAT SANDY DESERT

AUSTRALIA

GIBSON DESERT

GREAT VICTORIA DESERT

Darling

GREAT DIVIDING RANGE

GREAT AUSTRALIAN BIGHT

TASMANIA

TASMAN SEA

NORTH ISLAND

NEW ZEALAND

SOUTH ISLAND

Eucalyptus woodlands
The nectar and pollen of eucalyptus trees provide food for birds such as this Rainbow Lorikeet and many species of honeyeater, while parrots eat the seeds.

TYPICAL BIRDS
Here are just a few examples of typical birds from the most important habitats of Australasia. These range from rain forests, to drier eucalyptus woodlands and grasslands, to deserts, scrubland, lakes, rivers, and swamps. You can find out more about the birds of Australasia on the next few pages.

Rain forests
There are 37 species of birds of paradise, such as this Count Raggiana's, living in New Guinea's lush rain forests. Four more species live in Australia's rain forests.

Swamps
Birds such as the Brolga nest in swamps, which provide shelter from predators and are a source of fish and other food. Swamp birds include bitterns, egrets, herons, and ibises.

Scrublands
Butcherbirds, such as this Grey Butcherbird, as well as bell magpies and currawongs, all belong to the same family, found only in the scrublands of Australia and New Guinea.

Lakes and rivers
Waterbirds, such as this Black Swan, as well as ducks, and geese, feed and nest in freshwater habitats.

Deserts
Chats, such as this Orange Chat and some parrots and pigeons, manage to survive in deserts. They wander over large areas to find water and nest after rainfall, when insects start to hatch and plants grow.

Islands
The Brown Kiwi is just one of many unique flightless birds that live only on the islands of New Zealand. They evolved at a time when there were few enemies to fly away from.

Woodland and Desert

MOST OF AUSTRALIA HAS a dry climate. Vast areas in the middle of the continent are covered by hot desert, grassland, and scrubland, called the bush or outback. Some birds, such as chats, grasswrens, parrots, and pigeons, manage to find enough seeds and fruits to survive there, although they have to fly long distances to find water. Birds of prey can also survive by feeding on the many desert reptiles and small marsupials (mammals with pouches).

In the southeast and southwest of Australia are woodlands where a variety of eucalyptus trees grow. Here the climate is generally cooler and wetter. Marshes sometimes form during the rainy season, providing food and nesting places for ibises, pelicans, black swans, and ducks. Honeyeaters and lorikeets feed on the nectar and pollen in the eucalyptus trees and flowering shrubs, such as grevilleas and banksias. Parrots use their strong bills to crack open seeds. As they feed, the birds help pollinate the flowers and spread their seeds. Birds that feed on insects also find a rich supply of food on the leaves and bark of the eucalyptus trees.

Sharp, pointed bill is used to stab reptiles, such as this snake.

Laughing Kookaburra
(*Dacelo novaeguineae*)
Length: 18 in (45 cm)

LAUGHING KOOKABURRA
This giant kingfisher is named for its loud hooting and chuckling call. The noisy display tells other birds to keep out of its territory. Several birds may join in the laughter, usually in the early morning or late afternoon. The Laughing Kookaburra is also called the "bushman's clock" because it wakes people in the bush at dawn. It sometimes comes to town and city gardens to eat the food that people leave out for it. It has also been known to raid goldfish ponds.

WESTERN SPINEBILL
The Western Spinebill uses its needle-thin curved bill to probe for nectar in flowers. Its long bill can reach inside tube-shaped flowers or push into stiff brushlike flowers, such as banksias. It sometimes hovers in front of flowers to drink the nectar, soaking it up with a brush at the tip of its tongue. This spinebill also eats some insects and soft fruit.

Western Spinebill
(*Acanthorhynchus superciliosus*)
Length: 6 in (15 cm)

A Western Spinebill feeds on nectar from the flowers of a red gum, which is a kind of eucalyptus.

Splendid Fairy Wren
(*Malurus splendens*)
Length: 5.5 in (14 cm)

This bird often cocks its tail when perched on a branch.

A male brown honeyeater feeds on a banksia flower. As honeyeaters feed, they pick up pollen dust on their feathers and carry it to other flowers.

Males have shiny bright blue feathers, in the breeding season. Females are much duller in color all year round.

SPLENDID FAIRY WREN
Pairs of splendid, or banded, fairy wrens nest in small groups, with extra birds helping feed and defend the young. The helpers are often young birds that have not yet left their parents and started to fend for themselves. They help their younger brothers and sisters survive.

MALLEE FOWL		TAWNY FROGMOUTH	
LAUGHING KOOKABURRA		SPLENDID FAIRY WREN	
WESTERN SPINEBILL		SUPERB LYREBIRD	
EMU			

GREAT SANDY DESERT — MACDONNELL RANGES — GIBSON DESERT — A U S T R A L I A — SIMPSON DESERT — GREAT VICTORIA DESERT — Lake Eyre — NULLARBOR PLAIN — Darling — FLINDERS RANGES — Murray — GREAT AUSTRALIAN BIGHT — CORAL SEA — GREAT DIVIDING RANGE — TASMAN SEA — BASS STRAIT — TASMANIA — SOUTHERN OCEAN

0 200 400 600 km
0 200 400 miles

TAWNY FROGMOUTH

With its speckled and streaked gray and brown feathers, the Tawny Frogmouth is well camouflaged against tree bark during the day. At night, it glides down from its perch to pounce on beetles, centipedes, frogs, and mice on the woodland floor. It snaps up insects from among the fallen leaves, with its huge wide bill. The tuft of stiff feathers at the base of the bill may help the bird (like a cat's whiskers) find its way or sense food in the dark.

The frogmouth looks like a dead branch when it keeps very still in this stiff upright position.

Tawny Frogmouth
(Podargus strigoides)
Length: 18 in (46 cm)

EMU

The Emu is the second largest bird in the world today, after the ostrich. Its wings are very small and it cannot fly, although it can run quickly on its long legs. To find enough to eat, an Emu may move vast distances in a year, after the rains. It also stores food as fat in its body and survives on this in hard times. Several females lay their eggs in a hollow in the ground, and the male looks after them.

Emu
(Dromaius novaehollandiae)
Length: 6 ft 6 in (2 m)
Height: 5 ft 11 in (1.8 m)

The Emu can run at up to 30 mph (48 kph) to escape danger.

Emus are related to ostriches, but they have three toes on each foot, whereas ostriches only have two toes.

MALLEE FOWL

The Mallee Fowl builds a huge nest mound of wet leaves and twigs covered with sand. The female lays her eggs in the middle of the mound. As the leaves and twigs rot, they give off heat; this keeps the eggs warm. The male keeps a constant check on the temperature by prodding it with his bill, making sure it is always at about 93°F (34°C). He piles on more sand to make the mound warmer or opens up the mound to cool it down. When the chicks hatch, they dig their own way out.

A male tests the temperature of the nest mound with his bill.

Mallee Fowl
(Leipoa ocellata)
Length: 2 ft (60 cm)

Strong feet dig in the sand.

This bird is named after the male's two outer tail feathers, which are shaped like a Greek musical instrument called a lyre.

SUPERB LYREBIRD

The male Superb Lyrebird dances and sings on mounds of soil to attract females for mating and to drive away rival males. He fans out his long tail and arches it forward over his head, to form a shimmering silvery curtain. His body is almost hidden underneath the towering tail. The female builds the nest. She looks after a single egg on her own until the young bird leaves the nest, when it is about seven weeks old.

Budgerigars may roam the outback in flocks of thousands searching for water. Wild budgerigars are mainly green and yellow, but different colors have been developed in the birds we keep as pets.

Superb Lyrebird
(Menura novaehollandiae)
Length: male (including tail) up to 3 ft 3 in (1 m)
Female: 1 ft 8 in (50 cm)

He runs and leaps speedily on long powerful legs.

53

Rain Forests

THE BIRDS OF THE lush rain forests of northeastern Australia resemble those of New Guinea more than those of the rest of Australia. The two regions were joined together for much of their history and have a similar warm, wet climate with rain all year round. Their rain forests are rich in fruit trees for birds to feed on.

New Guinea is the second largest island in the world, after Greenland. Its high mountains, deep isolated valleys, and lack of mammal enemies allowed a huge variety of birds to evolve there, including the spectacular bower birds and birds of paradise. There are also more kinds of kingfisher in New Guinea than anywhere else in the world.

VICTORIA CROWNED PIGEON

This is one of the largest pigeons in the world – the size of a large chicken. Despite their size, these pigeons nest up to 49 ft (15 m) high in the trees.

The male Victoria Crowned Pigeon bows his head during his courtship display, to show off his splendid crest to a female. At the same time, he fans his tail up and down and makes a booming call.

This pigeon flies up into trees and perches on branches to escape danger.

Victoria Crowned Pigeon
(*Goura victoria*)
Length: 2 ft 2 in (66 cm)

Rivers bordered by rain forest in northeastern Australia provide a very lush habitat for birds. This is in contrast to the dry, hot deserts at the center of the continent.

BOWERBIRDS

Bowerbirds are related to birds of paradise, but the male birds do not have such colorful and elaborate feathers. Instead, they build "bowers" – shelters made out of twigs – and decorate them with colorful objects often set on a moss lawn. Females choose to mate with the males that have the best bowers, then go off to build their nests hidden safely in the forest.

Satin Bowerbird
(*Ptilonorhynchus violaceus*)
Length:13 in (33 cm)

The "avenue" bower is decorated with blue objects, which the bird seems to prefer.

MacGregor's Gardener
(*Amblyornis macgregoriae*)
Length: 10 in (25.5 cm)

"Maypole" bower; this bird has a large orange crest.

Vogelkop Gardener
(*Amblyornis inornatus*)
Length: 12 in (30 cm)

This is a complex "hut" bower; the bird has no crest, and its feathers are a dull color.

DOUBLE-WATTLED CASSOWARY

This huge cassowary is the height and weight of a small human being. It uses the tall, horny casque on its head to push aside the tangled forest undergrowth. Its long, hairlike feathers protect its body and keep it from getting scratched. The Double-wattled Cassowary wanders around the rain forest, searching for seeds, berries, and fruits to eat. Its survival is threatened by the destruction of its forest home.

During courtship, the male makes booming calls, puffing out his throat to make the calls louder.

Powerful legs and long claws are used for defense – the cassowary cannot fly to escape enemies.

Double-wattled Cassowary
(*Casuarius casuarius*)
Length: 5 ft (1.5 m)
Weight: up to 121 lb (55 kg)

Stripes on the chick help camouflage it.

BLUE BIRD OF PARADISE

To show off to a female, the male Blue Bird of Paradise hangs upside down from a branch and spreads out his lacy flank plumes in a shimmering fan. His long tail streamers form arches over his body while he shivers and sways to and fro. At the same time, he makes a strange, grating call, which sounds rather like an electric drill. Each male displays alone in a special dance tree in a set of trees. The drab females choose to mate with the male that makes the best display.

Blue Bird of Paradise
(*Paradisaea rudolphi*)
Length: 12 in (30 cm)

Here is a male displaying to a female.

The male holds his tail up during the courtship display.

The male trails his tail feathers behind him when not displaying.

King Bird of Paradise
(*Cicinnurus regius*)
Length: 6 in (16 cm)
Length of male's tail:
6 in (14 cm)

KING BIRD OF PARADISE

The bright red feathers of the male King Bird of Paradise contrast with the dull brown of the female. The female's colors help camouflage her while she cares for her eggs and chicks. She collects all the food she needs for herself and her chicks in the rain forest, leaving the male free for his stunning courtship displays.

ECLECTUS PARROT

Male and female eclectus parrots are such different colors that they were once thought to be different species. Both have some green feathers for camouflage in the rain forest, but the female stands out more than her mate. She is the only female parrot that is brighter than the male. Eclectus parrots roost at night in groups of up to 80 birds. By day, they travel through the treetops, searching for fruits, nuts, nectar, and leaves to eat.

The feet have a strong, vicelike grip on branches.

Male

Female

Eclectus Parrot
(*Eclectus roratus*)
Length: 15 in (38 cm)

RED-BREASTED PYGMY PARROT

This unique parrot lives only in New Guinea and on some of the nearby islands, where there are no woodpeckers. As it clings to tree trunks, this parrot uses its spiny tail feathers for support – just like a real woodpecker. It feeds on lichens and fungi and may also eat other plants and insects.

Red-breasted Pygmy Parrot
(*Micropsitta bruijnii*)
Length: 4 in (9 cm)

The stiff tail is used as a prop.

NEW BRITAIN

NEW GUINEA

0 250 500 km

0 200 400 miles

ARAFURA SEA

SOLOMON ISLANDS

CORAL SEA

PACIFIC OCEAN

GULF OF CARPENTARIA

GREAT BARRIER REEF

A gang-gang cockatoo feasts on forest berries. This bird is known for its loud, creaky doorlike screech.

GREAT SANDY DESERT

VOGELKOP GARDENER	
SATIN BOWERBIRD	MACGREGOR'S GARDENER
DOUBLE-WATTLED CASSOWARY	ECLECTUS PARROT
RED-BREASTED PYGMY PARROT	KING BIRD OF PARADISE
BLUE BIRD OF PARADISE	VICTORIA CROWNED PIGEON

AUSTRALIA

New Zealand

NEW ZEALAND CONSISTS mainly of two large islands – North and South Island. North Island has a warm subtropical climate with active volcanoes, but South Island is colder, with glaciers, a long mountain range – the Southern Alps – and beech forests.

New Zealand does not have a great variety of bird species. This is mainly because of its isolated position. It separated from the other landmasses millions of years ago as a result of continental drift. The few species it has, however, are very unusual. This is because New Zealand had very few mammals when it drifted off on its own, so the birds there began to live like mammals, running about and nesting on the ground. Many birds, such as the Kiwi and the Weka, stopped flying altogether because there were no mammal enemies to escape from. Unfortunately, these flightless birds later became easy prey for stoats and other mammals that people introduced to the islands.

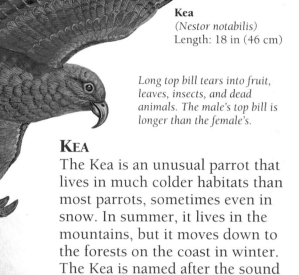

Kea
(*Nestor notabilis*)
Length: 18 in (46 cm)

Long top bill tears into fruit, leaves, insects, and dead animals. The male's top bill is longer than the female's.

KEA

The Kea is an unusual parrot that lives in much colder habitats than most parrots, sometimes even in snow. In summer, it lives in the mountains, but it moves down to the forests on the coast in winter. The Kea is named after the sound of its call, which echoes around the steep mountainsides. Both parents take care of the young until they are ready to leave the nest, after about 13 weeks.

LITTLE PENGUIN

The smallest penguin in the world lives around the coasts and islands of New Zealand. The Little Penguin, also known as the Blue or Fairy Penguin, spends the day fishing at sea, but it comes ashore at night. In the breeding season, little penguins pair up with the same mates at the same nest site year after year. They nest in a cave, among rocks or grass, or in a burrow.

Strong flippers and webbed feet are designed for swimming fast underwater.

Little Penguin
(*Eudyptula minor*)
Height: 16 in (40 cm)

NORTH ISLAND

TASMAN SEA

PACIFIC OCEAN

BAY OF PLENTY

EAST CAPE

RAUKUMARA RANGE

Lake Taupo

HAWKE BAY

Rangitikei

RUAHINE RANGE

NEW ZEALAND

COOK STRAIT

TARARUA RANGE

TASMAN MTS

SOUTH ISLAND

SOUTHERN ALPS

Rakaia

CANTERBURY PLAINS

Waitaki

TASMAN SEA

PACIFIC OCEAN

STEWART ISLAND

0   50   100   150 km
0   50   100 miles

	KIWI		KEA
	WRYBILL		TUI
	KAKAPO		LITTLE PENGUIN
	WEKA		

The bill curves to the right, but the bird holds its head to the left as it feeds.

Wrybill
(*Anarhynchus frontalis*)
Length: 20 cm (8 in)

WRYBILL

The Wrybill is named after its strange crooked, or wry, bill, which bends to the right at the tip, although no one is quite sure why this is so. The Wrybill is a kind of wading bird related to the plover. It spends the winter on the seashores of North Island and migrates to South Island in summer to breed on the shingle of large river beds. The bird and its eggs are well camouflaged among the stones.

Many seabirds, such as these pied oystercatchers, nest on the beaches and coasts of New Zealand. Others rest and feed there on migration to and from the Antarctic.

Tui
(*Prosthemadura novaeseelandiae*)
Length: 12 in (31 cm)

White throat tuft bobs up and down as the bird sings. Females have smaller throat tufts than those of males.

Tuis often gather in large numbers where there is a rich food supply.

TUI
The Tui is nicknamed the "parson bird" because the white tuft of feathers on its throat looks like the white collar worn by Christian parsons or vicars. Tuis are a kind of honeyeater; they use their brush-tipped tongues to lap up nectar from flowers. These noisy birds fly at high speed. In the breeding season, males make spectacular dives to impress females. They roll and loop-the-loop as they hurtle downward.

Strong wings help the bird keep its balance as it walks about.

WEKA
The inquisitive Weka cannot fly despite its well-developed wings. It feeds on all kinds of food, from grass, seeds, and fruit to mice, birds, eggs, and beetles. It even steals food from garbage cans near houses. Wekas have been introduced to some of New Zealand's smaller islands and have caused serious problems – they have damaged the plants and killed off many other birds that live on the ground. But they are also useful because they are good at killing the rats that attack New Zealand's rare birds.

This race of Weka lives only on South Island.

Weka
(*Gallirallus australis*)
Length: 1 ft 9 in (53 cm)

Powerful feet are designed for running fast when hunting or trying to escape enemies.

The high flat lands of North Island are covered with tree ferns and lush forests. Some tree ferns reach heights of up to 50 ft (15 m).

Kakapo
(*Strigops habroptilus*)
Length: 2 ft 1 in (63 cm)

Green feathers blend into a background of ferns and other forest plants and help camouflage the bird.

BROWN KIWI
The Brown Kiwi cannot fly and behaves more like a mammal than a bird. It comes out at night and stalks through bushes and leaves in the forests, sniffing out food with nostrils on the tip of its long bill, as a badger does in European forests. It is rare for a bird to have such a good sense of smell. The Brown Kiwi is covered with thick shaggy feathers, so it looks furry, like a mammal. The feathers help protect it from thorny bushes.

Long thin bill is used for probing for food such as earthworms, insects, spiders, and berries.

Brown Kiwi
(*Apteryx australis*)
Length: 1 ft 8 in (50 cm)

Strong legs are built for running; powerful claws can scratch for food.

KAKAPO
The Kakapo is one of the rarest parrots in the world. It lives on the ground and only comes out at night. It is too heavy to fly, with a thick layer of fat under its skin that makes up about 40 percent of its body weight. In the breeding season, males gather at special places in the forest and make loud, booming calls that carry for up to 1/2 mile (1 km). To make the calls louder, they dig a hollow under tree roots (which works like a megaphone). They also blow up their bodies with air, like a balloon.

Antarctica

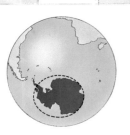

ANTARCTICA IS THE coldest and windiest place on Earth. Unlike the Arctic, which is an ocean surrounded by land, Antarctica is a huge area of land surrounded by ocean. Most of the land is covered with ice. With little rain or snow, there is hardly any fresh water for birds to drink.

In these harsh conditions, only two land birds manage to survive. Both are sheathbills – a type of bird related to a pigeon. The rest are seabirds, which have denser feathers than those of most land birds, to keep them warm. They are better at flying in stormy weather. In summer, some of the ice around the coasts melts, and millions of seabirds, such as albatrosses, petrels, penguins, and shearwaters, come ashore to lay eggs and raise their young. The Antarctic summer lasts only about four months, when it is light most of the time. During winter, most of the birds leave Antarctica and roam widely over the southern oceans in search of food.

Kelp gulls fly slowly and often glide, with their long wings stretched out.

KELP GULL

The huge Kelp Gull, or Dominican Gull, is the only gull that stays in the Antarctic all year round. Kelp gulls are good at fishing, but they also eat shellfish, dead animals, and the eggs and young of other birds. They sometimes carry shellfish up into the air and drop them onto rocks to break them open. Both parents sit on the eggs for about a month to keep them warm. The chicks can fly when they are about 5-6 weeks old.

Kelp Gull
(*Larus dominicanus*)
Length: 1 ft 10 in (58 cm)
Wingspan: 4 ft 3 in (130 cm)

Shags grow wispy crests during the breeding season.

Jagged hooked bill firmly grasps slippery fish.

Gentoo penguins and a few imperial shags nest on rocky islands around Antarctica in summer. Female gentoo penguins lay their eggs as soon as the snow melts in spring.

IMPERIAL SHAG

The Imperial Shag has webbed feet for swimming. Its feathers soak up water, so its weight increases, and it can sink and dive more easily. It has to spread out its wings to dry after a swim. The Imperial Shag nests in huge colonies on sheltered coastal ledges or among rocks. The helpless young are more likely to survive where there are large numbers of adults to drive away attackers. The nest is made of a pile of seaweed, stuck together with the birds' droppings, called "guano."

Imperial Shag
(*Phalacrocorax atriceps*)
Length: 2 ft 4 in (72 cm)

Huge hooked bill gobbles up fish or squid.

Large eyes search for food out at sea.

During the courtship display, the birds face one another, make groaning noises, snap their bills open and shut, and fence with their bills.

Wandering Albatross
(*Diomedea exulans*)
Wingspan: 11 ft 10 in (3.6 m)

WANDERING ALBATROSS

This magnificent albatross has the largest wingspan of any bird alive today. On its long, narrow wings, it glides effortlessly over the southern oceans at great speed, using air currents rising off the waves to lift it up into the air. It comes to the Antarctic islands only to nest. The chicks stay in the nest for almost a year before they grow all their feathers for flying. The parents feed out at sea, coughing up some of this food for the chicks to eat. Both adults and young can spray the sticky, smelly, oily food mixture up to 6 ft (2 m), to drive away enemies such as the Great Skua.

Snowy Sheathbill
(*Chionis alba*)
Length: 16 in (41 cm)

Although sheathbills fly well, they spend most of their time on the ground.

SNOWY SHEATHBILL
The Snowy, or Yellow-Billed, Sheathbill has a varied diet that changes with the seasons. In winter, it eats dead fish, shrimp-like krill, and limpets on the shoreline. In summer, it lurks near seal and penguin colonies and feeds on seal dung, weak or injured young seals and penguins, and penguin eggs. It also picks up food scraps from the garbage dumps of the many scientific bases in Antarctica.

Emperor Penguin
(*Aptenodytes forsteri*)
Length: 3 ft 9 in (1.1 m)

ANTARCTIC CIRCLE

ANTARCTICA

0   300   600   900 km

0   300   600 miles

WEDDELL SEA

ANTARCTIC PENINSULA

RONNE ICE SHELF

AMERY ICE SHELF

FLOOD RANGE

ROSS ICE SHELF

ROSS SEA

PRINCE ALBERT MTS

SOUTHERN OCEAN

KELP GULL
ADÉLIE PENGUIN
GIANT PETREL
IMPERIAL SHAG
SNOWY SHEATHBILL
EMPEROR PENGUIN
WANDERING ALBATROSS

EMPEROR PENGUIN
The enormous Emperor Penguin comes ashore at the start of the dark Antarctic winter and walks far inland to its nesting colonies, called rookeries. The female lays one large egg, then returns to the sea to feed. For about eight weeks, the male rests the egg on his feet and covers it with a flap of skin from his abdomen to keep it warm, like a tea cosy covering a pot of tea. During these freezing cold months, the male cannot eat and hardly moves. The female returns when the egg is due to hatch.

This is a young bird. Adults are mottled gray on the head, face, and underparts.

Giant Petrel
(*Macronectes giganteus*)
Length: 2 ft 11 in (90 cm)

GIANT PETREL
These birds are nicknamed "stinkers" because of their unpleasant smell and because they feed on dead animals, such as seals and whales. Like vultures, they use their massive bills to rip open the bodies of dead animals. Giant petrels also kill other petrels, as well as penguins and albatrosses, with their powerful hooked bills.

Flippers like oars "row" through the water.

Adélie penguins often dive into the sea from a favorite spot. They have to keep a lookout for leopard seals, which try to catch and eat them.

Adélie penguin
(*Pygoscelis adeliae*)
Length: 70 cm (2 ft 4 in)

ADÉLIE PENGUIN
Adélie and emperor penguins are the only two penguins that can survive on the frozen Antarctic continent. In spring, Adélie penguins march inland from the sea to their rookeries. These may contain more than a million birds. To mate, the birds usually return to the same rookery in which they were born. They greet their mates with a special courtship display, stretching their heads and necks up, beating their wings, and making drumming and braying calls.

Travelers of the World

Every year nearly half of all the birds in the world set off on journeys to find food, water, more space, or a warmer or cooler place. These regular journeys are called migration, from the Latin word *migrare*, meaning to go from one place to another. Migration usually takes place at night, but some birds, such as swallows, migrate during the day. Migration journeys are often very dangerous for birds, and millions never reach their destinations. They may run out of energy or be unable to find enough food to keep going. Many migrants are also killed by bad weather or by people and predators lying in wait along traditional routes.

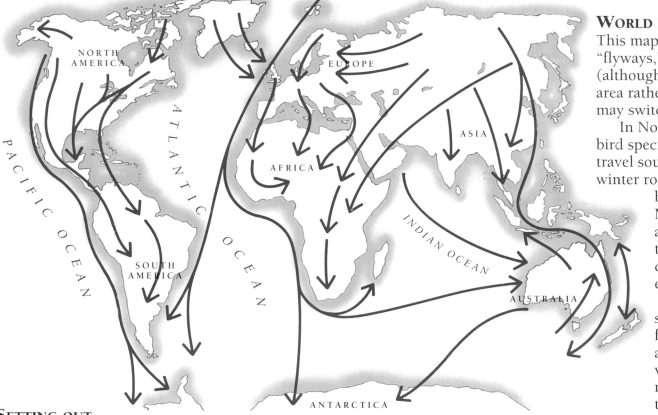

WORLD MIGRATION ROUTES

This map shows the main routes, or "flyways," that birds follow on migration (although birds generally move over a wide area rather than a narrow path, and they may switch from one flyway to another).

In North America, two-thirds of all the bird species that spend the summer there travel south for the winter. Another major winter route is from Europe to Africa. Many birds prefer to avoid crossing the Mediterranean Sea because there are no rising air currents to help them soar and glide along. So they cross it at its narrowest points – for example, by the Strait of Gibraltar.

The center of huge continents, such as Asia, has many good places for birds to feed and nest in spring and summer. But these areas get very cold in winter, so many birds migrate from the heart of Asia to the coasts.

SETTING OUT

Before migration, birds eat as much as they can to build up fat reserves in their bodies, to give them enough energy to keep going. They usually grow new feathers for the journey too. Birds know when to migrate because of changes in the weather. They also have a biological "clock" inside their brain that responds to changes in daylight hours. As the days get shorter in autumn, birds such as these barn swallows become restless and get ready to set off by gathering in flocks.

As they migrate, swallows feed on flying insects, to keep up their strength.

Barn Swallow
(Hirundo rustica)

Swallows have long pointed wings for fast and powerful flight. It takes them five or six weeks to fly from Europe to Africa.

FINDING THE WAY

There is still a lot we do not understand about how birds find their way, or navigate, on migration. They seem to know instinctively which way to go because many young birds make migration journeys for the first time without the help of adults.

Birds also steer by the Sun, the Moon, and the stars, and by the Earth's magnetic field. A few birds, such as shearwaters and petrels, pick up scents carried by the wind and use these to navigate their way across open oceans. Birds that migrate by day probably find their way year after year by following familiar landmarks, such as river valleys, mountain ranges, and coastlines.

FINDING OUT ABOUT MIGRATION

To learn how far birds migrate and where they go, scientists put metal or plastic rings on birds' legs. The rings are numbered or color-coded and have an address on them. It is then possible to identify individual birds and keep records of their migration movements. Another way of tracking birds' movements over shorter distances is by using a radio collar, like the one this Short-eared Owl is wearing.

THE JOURNEY

Birds use a lot of energy for continuous flapping flight, so on long journeys they have to try and conserve their strength. Some, such as common cranes, fly in a V-formation so that the birds following the leader do not use up as much energy pushing aside the air as they fly. Others, such as white storks, make use of rising hot air currents – called thermals – to glide and soar without using up any energy. Seabirds glide on currents that rise off the ocean waves. Some birds can build up enough stores of body fat to fly non-stop over deserts for four days; others have to stop and feed every day.

Common cranes migrate by day and by night from Europe to Africa. They are strong fliers and can cross the Mediterranean at its widest point.

Common Crane
(Grus grus)

Short-tailed Shearwater
(Puffinus tenuirostris)

Birds often migrate in flocks of thousands of birds. Flying in a V-formation helps these common cranes save energy on a long journey.

MIGRATION FROM NORTH TO SOUTH

In the northern hemisphere, where much of the land is covered with ice and snow in winter, many birds, including the Lesser Golden-Plover, migrate. They spend summer in the north and fly south to warmer places for the winter, returning north again in spring.

Very few landbirds migrate in the opposite direction – from the southern to the northern hemisphere. But several southern seabirds, such as the Short-tailed Shearwater, do migrate over the Equator to the oceans of the northern hemisphere for the summer because the climate is warmer and there is more food there.

Lesser Golden-Plover
(Pluvialis dominica)

This shearwater nests in Tasmania, in Australia, and on islands in the South Pacific Ocean. In April, it flies north to Japan and east to the United States, before heading south again for the winter.

The Lesser Golden-Plover nests in the tundra of Alaska and northern Canada and migrates down to the pampas of South America for the winter.

AMAZING MIGRANTS

Arctic Tern
(Sterna paradisaea)

Champion migrant
Every year, the Arctic Tern flies from the top to the bottom of the world and back – a distance of about 22,000 miles (36,000 km).

High fliers
Most birds fly below 300 ft (91 m) on migration, but some cross high mountains. Condors migrate at 6,035 m 19,800 ft (6,035 m) in the Andes, and geese in the Himalayas migrate at heights of more than 31,168 ft (9,500 m).

Weight-watcher
Small birds, such as the Blackpoll Warbler, may double their weight before migrating, in order to "fuel" their journey.

Tiny migrant
Most hummingbirds do not migrate far, but the Ruby-throated Hummingbird travels up to 2,000 miles (3,200 km) across the eastern USA and the Gulf of Mexico to Central America. Experts do not know how such tiny birds have the energy for such a long flight.

Ruby-throated Hummingbird
(Archilochus colubris)

Birds in Danger

BIRDS ARE ENDANGERED ALL OVER the world. More than 1,000 bird species, about 10 percent of all known birds, are in danger of dying out. The parrot family is the most threatened group, with more than 70 species at risk. Many birds die out naturally as a result of changes in the environment. New species develop to take their place. But people have speeded up this extinction process. They have increased the number of threats to bird survival by destroying habitats, causing pollution, hunting birds, and catching them to keep in cages. We urgently need to do more to help save the world's rare birds.

THREATENED BIRDS

These are some of the rarest birds in the world. In most cases there are fewer than 150 of each species left in the wild, although people are trying to save them in nature reserves or protected areas.

Eskimo Curlew
(*Numenius borealis*)
Americas

Ivory-billed Woodpecker
(*Campephilus principalis*)
Americas

Chatham Island Black Robin
(*Petroica traversi*)
New Zealand

Noisy Scrub-bird
(*Atrichornis clamosus*)
Australia

Gurney's Pitta
(*Pitta gurneyi*)
Thailand

White-tailed Sea Eagle
(*Haliaeetus albicilla*)
Europe

HABITAT DESTRUCTION

Dalmatian Pelican
(*Pelecanus crispus*)

This is by far the most serious threat to birdlife today. About two-thirds of the endangered birds in the world are threatened by the destruction of their habitat. Marshes and swamps have been drained and used for farms; grasslands have been ploughed up to grow crops or graze cattle; and forests have been cleared for their timber or to make way for farms, houses, and mines. For example, dalmatian pelicans (above) were once common in southeastern Europe and in the Russian Federation, Iran, and Turkey. They have now become an endangered species due to disturbance from people, and because of drainage of the rivers, lakes, deltas, and estuaries on which they nest. Rain forests are one of the richest habitats for birds, but more than half of the world's rain forests have already been destroyed and an area of rain forest about the size of a soccer pitch disappears every second.

HUNTING AND COLLECTING

Until about 60 years ago, many birds were hunted to obtain feathers, such as ostrich plumes, to decorate hats for the fashion trade. Millions of birds such as egrets were killed each year for their beautiful courtship plumes. In the past, people have also significantly reduced bird numbers by hunting them and collecting their eggs for food. For example, passenger pigeons were once the most abundant birds in the world. Huge flocks used to fill the skies. Yet in the 19th century, Europeans setting up home in North America killed millions of them. In less than 100 years, the Passenger Pigeon was extinct. Hunting birds for food is not as important today, but people still hunt birds for sport, especially waterbirds such as ducks and geese. Birds that follow the same routes on migration are easy targets for predators, including people.

Many of Asia's tropical rain forests have been cleared. This causes a great threat to Asian birdlife. The Japanese Crested Ibis, for example, almost died out due to destruction of its forest home; it is now a protected species.

Crested Ibis
(*Nipponia nippon*)

People collect fulmar eggs in the thousands, from breeding colonies off the coasts of Iceland. This need not threaten bird numbers, as long as the number of eggs taken is not too high.

Houbara Bustard
(*Chlamydotis undulata*)

The Houbara Bustard of Pakistan became rare because it was hunted and killed for sport.

Black Paradise Flycatcher
(Tersiphone corvina)

INTRODUCED SPECIES

As people have moved from place to place, they have brought with them a variety of animals, especially cats, dogs, rats, and birds, such as house sparrows. Introduced species cause particular problems on islands, such as Hawaii and New Zealand, where the native birds often have no defense against the new intruders. They attack the birds already living in a place, spread disease, and compete with them for food and space. Introduced species can also rapidly change the habitat of their new homes. The native birds usually cannot adapt to these rapid changes and soon die out. For example, black paradise flycatchers (above) were once found in large numbers throughout the Seychelles, but they are now found mainly on one island, and there are fewer than 100 left. They were driven out of other areas by rats and cats.

Takahe
(Notornis mantelli)

Stoat
(Mustela erminea)

Stoats were introduced into New Zealand to try to control the rising numbers of rats and other small mammals. Unfortunately, they raided the eggs and chicks of a rare flightless bird called the Takahe, which almost became extinct as a result.

THE END OF THE LINE

Some birds have died out completely. One example is the Dusky Seaside Sparrow. Until the 1940s, thousands of these small songbirds lived on the saltmarshes on the east coast of Florida, in the USA. Then, in the mid-1950s, Cape Canaveral and the NASA Space Center were built on these marshes, and dikes were constructed to stop the tidal flooding. The sparrows needed the floodwaters to provide food for their survival, so they soon began to die out. Some birds were protected in a wildlife refuge, but in 1975, fire destroyed their habitat, and no females have been seen since. The last 100 percent Dusky Seaside Sparrow died in 1989.

Dusky Seaside Sparrow
(Ammodramus maritimus nigrescens)

Caged songbird

TRADE IN CAGED BIRDS

Many people like to keep birds in cages as pets, for their beautiful color, their songs, and their company. Most of these birds are taken from Africa, Asia, and South America and bought by people in western countries. Small seed-eating songbirds make up about 80 percent of the trade, but about 600,000 parrots are also traded each year. Parrots fetch much higher prices than songbirds do.

The worst part of the trade is the large number of birds that die during capture, while waiting to be sold, or on their journey to a life in captivity. They are often tightly packed in boxes without food or water for their trip. For every 10 birds caught in the wild, only about one ever reaches a pet shop.

POLLUTION

Birds are threatened by all sorts of chemicals that pollute the air, land, or water – from oil and acid rain, to pesticides and factory wastes. Oil spills at sea occur after shipping accidents or when tankers illegally wash out their tanks. The oil causes great damage to seabirds. It makes their feathers stick together, so they can no longer keep out the cold or wet, and it prevents them from diving for food. Birds may also be poisoned by swallowing the oil when they preen their feathers. When birds such as this Jackass Penguin (above) are caught in an oil spill, they have to be cleaned very swiftly; otherwise they will die from cold and hunger.

Acid rain, caused when chemicals from vehicle exhaust fumes and power stations mix with water in the air, is also a problem for birds. The rain falls on forests and lakes, damaging or killing the water birds or the food they eat.

WHAT WE CAN DO TO HELP

Mauritius Pink Pigeon
(Nesoenas mayeri)

The world's rare birds need our help if they are to survive. Birds are closely linked to all the other wildlife on the planet, so if there are problems for birds, these serve as a warning of problems for plants, animals, and people. We can help in many ways:

● Set aside areas of land and water as nature reserves or wildlife sanctuaries, where birds will be protected from disturbance, hunting, and introduced species.

● Set up more artificial feeding areas for birds, to help them survive in harsh climates. The machine shown below distributes food for trumpeter swans in North America during the winter. This keeps them alive when the lakes containing the water plants they feed on freeze over.

● Breed rare birds in captivity and release them back into the wild. Numbers of the Mauritius Pink Pigeon were built up in this way.

● Ban the hunting of rare species, and stop birds from being shot on migration.

● Stop keeping wild birds in cages, and keep birds bred in captivity instead.

● Reduce the amount of pollution, especially from oil spills and pesticides.

● Carry out research to find out as much as possible about how birds live, so we can plan the best ways to conserve them.

● Pass international laws to protect endangered species.

● Join conservation organizations to protest, raise money, and make other people aware of the problems.

INDEX

ACKNOWLEDGMENTS

Dorling Kindersley would like to thank the following:
David Gillingwater, Rachael Foster, and Mark
Thompson for design assistance, and Lynn Bresler for
compiling the index.

Picture research Clive Webster

Maps Andrew MacDonald

Globes and diagrams John Hutchinson

Cartographic consultant Roger Bullen

Bird symbols Heather Blackham

Photo credits
a=above, b=below, c=centre, l=left, r=right, t=top
Bridgeman Art Library: 24cl.
Bruce Coleman: 53bc;
Erwin and Peggy Bauer 16bc Alain Compost 62bl;
Gerald Cubitt 37tr, 41tl, 43tc, 47tc, 63c;
Peter Davey 39tl; Christer Fredriksson 35tc;
Jeff Foot Productions 11tc, 63bc;
Michael Freeman 21cl; Frances Furlong 50br;
Giorgio Gualgo 25bl; Pekka Helo 28c;
Joy Langsbury 17c; Wayne Lankinen 11tl;
L C Marigo 23c; Fco Marquez 30tc;
Dieter and Mary Plage 45br; G D Plage 45tl;

Fritz Prenzel 51tr; Hans Reinhard 54tr;
Gary Retherford 19bl; Leonard Lee Rue 58cl;
John Shaw 9tr, 12c; Kim Taylor 33c;
Norman Owen Tomalin 26bc; Nicholas de Vore 43tl;
G Ziesler 22bc.
The Image Bank: 7tl;
James Carmichael 20br; Per Eide 27tl;
Don King 42cr; Peter Muller 27tc.
Frank Lane: C Carvalho 35tr; Tom and Pam Gardner;
52c; A R Hamblin 18bl; Eric and David Hosking 35tl;
40br; S Jonasson 62bc; S Maslowski 13tc; R van
Nostrand 15tr; F Polking 24cr; P Reynolds 61tl;
L Robinson 55bl; J Wisniewski 36br;

NHPA: Anthony Bannister 38br, 39c;
V Garcia Canseco 31cr; B Chudleigh 57tl;
J S Gifford 32cl; Melvin Grey 33cr;
Stephen Krasemann 14cr;
Orion Press 49tc; Otto Rogge 50bl, 57cr;
Morten Strange 47cr;
Roger Tidman 29cr.
Oxford Scientific Films:
Kjell Sandved 10br.
Planet Earth Pictures / John Waters /
Bernadette Spiegel 7c.
South American Pictures: 11tr.